Praise for Eden Collinsworth's

Behaving Badly

"Morality is a complicated subject, but Eden Collinsworth breaks it down. . . . Her analysis is surprisingly light and fun."　　　　　　　　　　　　　　　　　　　　*—Bustle*

"Fascinating. . . . A refreshing read."　　　　　*—Big Think*

"Regardless of the era, vice is a tale as old as time, and author Eden Collinsworth works wonders to produce a fresh spin on one of humanity's oldest dichotomous positions, morality."　　　　　　　　　　　　　　　　　　*—PopMatters*

"Every day we see and hear stories of bad behavior in sports, business, and politics, in which bad people with no moral compass seem to succeed. . . . This extraordinary, thought-provoking book by Eden Collinsworth makes us stop and consider who we are and who we want to be."

—Ed Rollins,
former U.S. presidential adviser

"Eden Collinsworth doesn't pull her punches as she explores the shifting moral landscape of our times. *Behaving Badly* is as insightful as it is hilarious."　　　　—Amanda Foreman,
author of *Georgiana: Duchess of Devonshire*

Eden Collinsworth

Behaving Badly

Eden Collinsworth is a former media executive and business consultant. She was president of Arbor House Publishing Co. and founder of the Los Angeles–based monthly lifestyle magazine *Buzz*, before becoming a vice president at Hearst Corporation. She served as the chief of staff at the East-West Institute, a global think tank; in 2011—after writing a bestselling book in China for Chinese businesspeople on Western deportment—she launched Collinsworth & Associates, a Beijing-based consulting company, which specialized in intercultural communication. The author of *I Stand Corrected: How Teaching Western Manners in China Became Its Own Unforgettable Lesson*, she currently lives in London.

www.edencollinsworth.com

Also by Eden Collinsworth

*I Stand Corrected: How Teaching Western Manners
in China Became Its Own Unforgettable Lesson*

It Might Have Been What He Said

*Behaving
Badly*

Behaving Badly

· ·

THE NEW MORALITY IN POLITICS,

SEX, AND BUSINESS

Eden Collinsworth

ANCHOR BOOKS
A Division of Penguin Random House LLC
New York

The Library of Congress has cataloged the Doubleday edition as follows:
Names: Collinsworth, Eden, author.
Title: Behaving badly : the new morality in politics, sex, and business /
Eden Collinsworth.
Description: First edition. | New York : Nan A. Talese/Doubleday, [2017] |
Includes bibliographical references.
Identifiers: LCCN 2016038550940
Subjects: LCSH: Ethics, Modern—21st century. | Conduct of life. |
Business ethics. | Sexual ethics. | Political ethics.
Classification: LCC BJ320 .C65 2017 | DDC 170.9/051—dc23
LC record available at https://lccn.loc.gov/2016038947

Anchor Books Trade Paperback ISBN: 978-1-101-97081-2
eBook ISBN: 978-0-385-54094-0

Author photograph © Sim Canetty-Clarke
Book design by Michael Collica

www.anchorbooks.com

Printed in the United States of America
10   9   8   7   6   5   4   3   2   1

For Susannah Fiennes and Tessa Keswick,
and in memory of William

"Don't, for Christ's sake, get into the Goddam morality of this."

NOTE TO THE READER

The consideration of morality cannot survive without a great deal of humility and some degree of humor. My intention is that both be brought to bear here, for I am not an ethicist or a social scientist and this is not an academic debate on the topic of morality but an adventurous search for its modern-day relevance.

CONTENTS

PROLOGUE

A great many people think they are thinking when
they are merely rearranging their prejudices.

*—attributed to William James, nineteenth-century
American philosopher, psychologist, and author*

It began as a lively conversation.

That was before disagreement made itself known and
caused tempers to flare. Manners were breached. One person
stormed out of the room. Another was reduced to tears.

My mother—European by birth and old-world in her
convictions—was an extremely correct woman, the kind who
became confused when someone who didn't know her well
nonetheless called her by her first name. When I phoned to
debrief her about my friends' bad behavior, she was embarrassed for me.

"And this took place in your apartment?" she asked, trying
to get her bearings. "What on earth caused such a scene?"

"We were talking about morality," I told her.

"I can't imagine why you would encourage that kind of
discussion," she said, more accusation than query.

"It wasn't *me*" was my childish claim before ignominiously
placing the blame on my dinner guests. "Someone said something, and the next thing I knew, it was out of my control."

Always and immaculately in control, my mother told me

that it is the obligation of the guests to ensure that the host has no regrets for having invited them but it is the duty of the host to make sure the guests are not made uncomfortable in conversation. The fault, she informed me, was entirely mine for allowing provocation to introduce itself at the dining table. Bad behavior should never be given an opportunity to declare itself, she said, and not to lose sight of the broader issue, she reminded me that moral conduct must always hold its ground.

My mother was right.

But how is one sure what constitutes bad behavior, given the shifting tectonic plates under that defining issue? More fundamentally, where does one find solid moral ground on what is proving to be the porous bedrock of our twenty-first century?

"Civility clears a path toward morality" was how my mother concluded our phone conversation, as if it were all I needed to know.

No single generation can claim a peerless contribution to ethical behavior, but in my mother's time morality was a rule book: some parts enshrined as decent behavior; others, implicit. Sins were laid bare and bad behavior had far-reaching and lasting consequences.

That is no longer the case. What were clearly designated ethics have been blurred: in politics, with our leaders, for whom we have less and less respect but are willing, more and more, to accept that their bad deeds have mitigating factors; with the Wall-Street-take-all mentality in business, where it has become difficult to define cheating, lying, and stealing; in popular entertainment, with morally prismatic antiheroes operating in a stylish gray zone; and in our daily lives, whose churning technology grants permission to act in ways we would not necessarily act without it. For the first time in history, we have the skills and the knowledge to modify ourselves, both biologically and digitally, yet we struggle with the fundamental conceit of living successfully in the here and now with our fellow humans.

In this unsettling era, moral variables are being shaped less by ideals than by global markets, so perhaps we should remind ourselves who is holding the checkbook. In the 1920s, British firms owned 40 percent of the global stock of foreign direct investment; by the 1960s, America had assumed the mantle. Despite its growing pains from recent state-dictated reforms, China—whose economy in the last twenty-five years has quintupled—is likely to be next.

The population of China is 1.3 billion (compared with America's 318.9 million). Its culture—formed over two and a half millennia—embraces a Confucian perspective, which is in stark contrast to the linear rationalism attributed to Western belief. Confucius's analects concentrate on the practical rather than the theoretical; they advise against reducing morality to a universal truth. Unlike the West, where Judeo-Christian ethics designate a nonnegotiable right and wrong, the Chinese do not adhere to absolutes. This means that one in five of the world's current population believes that there is no single way of being wrong and many ways of being right.

Where does that leave the rest of us?

We in the West would like to believe that individual freedom determines our choices, but in reality we are ruled by our culture and the prevailing time in which we live. Since he was old enough to understand my words, I tried to teach my son the difference between right and wrong, but the plain fact is that his take on morality wasn't instilled by me as much as it was dictated by the profound changes during the course of his life: changes brought about by advancements in technology and science I don't fully understand and my mother could not have imagined.

ARE THESE CHANGES pointing us in the right moral direction? I'm not sure. I asked others. It turns out that most of them aren't sure either, and I decided that the question was worthy of more investigation. I thought that, if I spent a year trying to discover where and how morality is changing, I might be able to chart where it's going.

I'm not an obvious navigator for this kind of exploration: a peripatetic career has moved me in disparate directions, none toward advanced academic degrees. And although I have lived in different countries, my life has unfolded in cities. Those who live in cities have a tendency to circulate within the confines of their socioeconomic class or occupational orbits, so there's a good chance I have a narrower outlook than is ideal for what I'm proposing to do. That said, I shall do my best to avoid prejudices, marshaling the facts as they are, not as I wish them to be.

Here are a few more disclosures: I admire those of faith but believe that religion should be kept far away from as many non-spiritual things as humanly possible. I have an abiding affection for the offbeat, but I aspire—however imperfectly—to civility. I can't imagine an absolute moral man or woman, nor can I understand why anyone would wish that state of absolute being. In fact, I'm inclined to agree with Henry David Thoreau, whose suggestion is not to be too moral a being. "You may cheat yourself out of much life so," he warned.

From this information, you are likely to decide that I've wandered to the far ends of orthodoxy and that this makes me a willful person. That could be. But mine is not the kind of willfulness that challenges the necessity of morality or the purpose of ethics. Nietzsche—the "God Is Dead" nihilist—insisted that "man has connected all things in existence with morals, and dressed up the world in a garb of ethical significance. The day will come when all this will be . . . utterly valueless."

I'm sorry, but no. Morality is at the core of who we are, and ethics enable us to function in societal groups. So, no, my intention here is not to argue whether there is a need for morality but to map its landscape.

Perhaps you are already of one mind or the other about what constitutes moral behavior or—like me—in possession of an inward sense of what is fundamentally good or bad but not sure how either applies anymore. For the purpose of this endeavor, we might think of ourselves as flaneurs, strolling down the broad avenues of history, pausing to ask the ethical standard-bearers how they judged good behavior. We have begun this journey with a question, and there's no guarantee that we won't end with one, but along the way it seems only fair that we give bad behavior an opportunity to explain itself.

PART ONE

Confronting the Unreliable
Provenance of Morals

WHEREIN I BEGIN WITH THE
DEFINITION OF THE WORD

Man is happy when he is able to
know the cause of things.

—Virgil

No one gets to a certain age without having made a few basic decisions on how to be in the world. I decided some time ago that it's okay to be a little afraid. That might explain why—speaking not a word of Chinese and carrying with me a single packed suitcase—I left New York to move to Beijing and collaborate with a major Chinese book publisher on a Western etiquette guide for the Chinese.

It wasn't the first time that I pursued an unlikely proposition. Years ago, with no experience in either raising money or magazine publishing, and at the time eight months pregnant, I decamped New York to launch a magazine in Los Angeles, a city I hardly knew.

GERTRUDE STEIN SUGGESTED that "there is no *there* there" to Southern California, but it was a beacon of clarity compared with the incoherence that became my experience in China. What began as a straightforward proposition to write a book turned into something else entirely when the government censor appeared on the scene.

It would be an understatement to say that China stage-manages the exposure of Western ideas to its citizens. The government's censor (which, in Orwellian doublespeak, is called the Ministry of Information) demonstrated just how thorough is its process: it withheld the publication of my book for an innocuous inclusion of the word "Muslim" in the chapter that instructed readers on appropriate greetings when traveling in foreign lands.

A single word kept the book out of the stores and me in China longer than expected. When, finally, the censor granted permission for the book to be published, no one was more surprised than I that it became a best seller in mainland China.

These circumstances and their outcome made me aware that though the Chinese wanted to learn how to do business with the West, Western values were beside the point. But there was more to it than that: just as significant a realization at the time was that my personal values were becoming less and less relevant in my own country.

Cultures adjust their societal expectations according to change, and while most Americans are not opposed to change, the British are known to be reluctant, even when they have no choice but to accept it. This is probably why that country's Ministry of Justice only recently removed the offense of "being an incorrigible rogue" from its statute book.

Despite their class-tinged society, Britons seem to me to possess a sense of fairness; and, regardless of their squeamish avoidance of the sentimental, I've always thought them congenial. Artists, chefs, writers, architects, and scientists have landed from foreign shores to make London a culturally open capital whose inhabitants can appear at the Speakers' Corner near Marble Arch to publicly address any number of issues: Muhammad, UFOs, processed food, and Jesus are only a few of the topics I've heard deliberated there, and, if not fully coherent, all of those debates remained civil.

I'm not as convinced as my mother that civility clears a path to morality; indeed, I've seen a fair share of the opposite. But because the British appear to be clinging to the hallmarks of grace and dignity (despite the tendency of their newspapers to be extremely rude), I came to the conclusion that the U.K. might have another few decades of civility left. So, rather than returning to America from China, I decided to move to London for the year I planned to map morality.

That decision was rendered irreversible when rules prevented me from subleasing my New York apartment longer than the year I was in China, giving me no choice but to sell the apartment. With that decision came the need for another: this one having to do with where I would live in London once I arrived.

Like most international cities these days, London primarily accommodates the rich, and so I was grateful when Simon, an English friend who lives there, alerted me to an affordably priced rental flat available in his neighborhood. Because it was within walking distance of almost everything I thought might be important to me, I wired a deposit based on little more information than the apartment's floor plan the broker sent.

The broker measured the flat's floor-to-ceiling windows and agreed to receive forty meters of yellow silk mailed from a state-run mill on the outskirts of Beijing so that during my last months living in China, draperies could be made in London while my possessions crossed the Atlantic by ship, stopping first in Amsterdam before docking in Southampton. They would be trucked to Wimpole Street in central London and uncrated in front of a large nineteenth-century house whose parlor floor had long ago been converted to what would be my home, seen for the first time when I arrived in front of it. The flat's enormous and purposeless dumbwaiter hinted at past glamour. High ceilings and handsome features made up for the almost impossibly narrow bathroom slivered from the flat's hallway. A sizable eat-in kitchen and a large bedroom overlooked leafy terraces in the back.

—

AS SOON AS I unpacked, I invited Simon for lunch to thank him for his role in my move to London, and despite my diminished state of sobriety from the champagne I managed to explain my plans to write a book about morality.

Simon has known me for a great many years, and that grants him the right to point out when I'm flirting with the ridiculous. Still, I'd just arrived in his country, and he wanted to be helpful, so, rather than pointing out the road signs to folly, he asked what I imagined I would discover at the end of my proposed journey.

"I'm not sure," I had to admit.

"Where will you begin?" he asked.

"I'm not sure of that either."

"Why not start with the definition of the word?" he suggested. "You might try looking in the vicinity of St. James's Square."

ST. JAMES'S SQUARE surrounds a leafy summer garden, in the center of which stands an equestrian statue of William III. He appears to be surveying the handsome congregation of the surrounding Georgian buildings that managed to survive being bombed during World War II. On the square's northwest corner is a slender edifice whose outward face suggests one of the several unassuming gentlemen's clubs that pepper the area.

A perfect place to start, I say to myself as I enter the reception area of the London Library. Only it's referred to not as a reception area but as the Issue Hall, and so dimly lit is it that I can barely make out the man sitting behind the front desk. Gray weather has taken hold of the morning, and filtering through the window is just enough pallid sunlight to convince the man that he need not turn on his desk lamp.

Good manners prevail here: the man at the desk reveals

himself to be extremely courteous. When asked about the accessibility of the books, he has a gentle way of informing me that I am standing in a private institution where only members can access the books. At least that's what I think he's said. Instead of calling them books, he referred to "the collections" as he handed me a membership application.

"We are known as a writer's library," the man points out with obvious pride, whereupon I quit the building feeling slightly less worthy than when I entered. As I walk home, my confidence is further eroded by blue plaques on the buildings I pass.

Launched by the Victorians 150 years ago, London's Heritage blue plaques scheme is believed to be the oldest of its kind. Set in motion by Henry Cole, inventor of the Christmas card, more than nine hundred blue plaques dot London, providing a historical link between an illustrious or notorious person and the building in which he or she once lived or worked.

Buildings displaying the uniform-size, round blue plaques can appear several to a block, and it happens that London's first plaque—commemorating Lord Byron's birthplace—is on a building not far from where I live. Directly across from my apartment on Wimpole Street is one pointing out what was once Elizabeth Barrett's home; down a block on the same street, a plaque designates what had been the workplace of Arthur Conan Doyle.

I pass dozens of blue plaques in the twenty minutes it takes me to walk home from St. James's Square, and by the time I arrive there, self-doubt about being granted library membership has set in. I look at the application to see exactly what is required to at least try.

Actually, it doesn't look that difficult, I tell myself as I read on. *Uh-oh.*

At the bottom of the page is a blank for the name of a "referee," a word I realize has more than a sports' connotation. Apparently, it will be necessary for me to designate a respectable person living in the United Kingdom, who can vouch for my character—this, I would guess, so the admission committee can safely conclude that I will not openly misbehave. I name as my London-based referee not Simon, who is an actor with a spotty relationship with authority, but Tessa, an exceedingly respectable friend, who has witnessed the disorderly side of me only on rare occasions and never in a public space.

Reading about morality in books is not necessarily the same as understanding it, and so, while waiting to hear about my membership at the London Library, I decide on more of a grassroots approach: I begin to write letters to people I know, and others I'd heard or read about, who might be willing to explain why and how they've chosen to follow the moral status quo, fight to protect it, or act in outright defiance of it. A series of introductions quickly lead to a man with whom I begin a correspondence. I suggest that we meet.

That I did any of this stunned Simon.

"Are you insane?" he demanded to know. "I thought you were researching morality at the London Library."

I told Simon that I intended to do that as well. I told him that this had come up unexpectedly and that it would be a missed opportunity if I didn't take advantage of it. I'm not insane, I told him.

He didn't believe me.

"No sane person asks someone who's killed another person to tea in her apartment to discuss morality!"

Thinking it best to lay out the facts, I informed Simon that there had been two.

" 'Two?' What are you talking about?"

"Two murders."

Simon hung up on me.

A few moments later, he phoned back.

"What in God's name were you thinking?"

I explained that I wanted to record my discussion, that I needed a private and quiet space, that I work from home, that home is private and quiet. I told Simon that the man had paid his dues and that I didn't see why I should think of an alternative place because of who he was.

"He might be out of prison—whether he's paid his dues is a question I suggest you ask the families of the two people he killed," was Simon's sharply worded reply.

British law limits what can be published about a person once he or she has been charged with a crime, and details of that crime are not often revealed after a criminal is released from prison. The man I was to meet referred to himself as Erwin James. It was not his birth name. He is a convicted murderer of two people.

MR. JAMES HADN'T volunteered any details in our correspondence, nor did I ask, but judging from the measured intelligence with which he expressed himself, I convinced myself that the murders must have been a crime of passion, that he murdered a certain way and for a certain reason.

It was only after Mr. James and I agreed to meet that I learned that the two murders were gruesome, committed separately and for no other purpose than to rob. Had I the courage, I would have given Simon the full story. Instead, I asked him not to argue with me.

"Fine. I won't argue. But if you insist on going ahead with this, I should be there," he said.

"That won't work," I told him.

"What do you mean it won't work?"

"It would change things."

"Who cares? Under the idiotic circumstances you've put yourself in, it's the only sensible thing to do."

"I realize what I've done. I've offered this man my goodwill. I won't take it back."

I waited through a long pause until Simon's indignation gave way to curiosity.

"What will you ask him?" he wanted to know.

ACCORDING TO A CONVICTED MURDERER, IT HAS TO DO WITH CHARACTER

Character is destiny.

—*Heraclitus*

I pressed the buzzer that released the front door lock, which allowed Mr. James into the building, and then I positioned myself on my floor's landing and leaned over the banister to spot any early signs of trouble.

The skylight provided a clear view of the man coming up the stairs: he appeared to be in his fifties and was densely built, neatly dressed, and carrying a knapsack. Rounding the staircase corner, he answered my scrutiny with his own analytically appraising gaze.

I introduced myself in the hallway.

A half smile emerged tentatively from his broad-featured face, one colonized by furrows, nicks, and striated lines.

"Please come in," I said, not sure that's what I actually wanted.

MY APARTMENT IS furnished with items gathered during my travels and considered curious by most people who visit. Displayed in the front hall is a crop of sorts purchased in India to ride an elephant, a Masai spear from Africa, a seven-foot snakeskin brought back from the Amazon, a Chinese opium pipe found in what is known as Beijing's Dirt Market, and a photograph of the king of Thailand taken when he was a boy and discovered in an old bookstore in Bangkok. Training his eyes straight ahead, Mr. James didn't so much as glance at the surroundings after he placed his knapsack near the coat closet.

I directed him to a comfortable armchair near the fireplace and sat down on the couch opposite. Between us was an ottoman, on which were a large Turkish tray with a pot of jasmine tea, a plate of dates, tangerines, and a recording device that had been switched on before I let him through the building's front door.

We both sat mutely and visibly uneasy until I began to explain my reasons for exploring the meaning of morality. Mr. James listened intently, frowning at the cup of tea he held in his hand rather than drinking from it.

The life he lived growing up lacked any stability—certainly not the type of stability that might foster morality, he told me.

"MY FEELING IS that morality is developed," he said. "I developed some part of mine, ironically, in prison, when I was encouraged into education. There was a psychologist who died shortly after I got out. I was never able to thank her properly, but her principles and her humanity made all the difference to me."

Hearing him use the word "humanity" lessened most—not all, but most—of the apprehension I was feeling. I asked if he thought he would have recognized the moral principles the psychologist possessed in a time before he committed murder.

"Probably not. I had such a dysfunctional life. It was corrupted with so much violence."

Mr. James was born to itinerant Scottish parents in an environment of deprivation, unemployment, and alcoholism, and his childhood was a bleak catalog of traumas. A prison psychologist described his family life as "brutal and rootless."

His mother was killed when he was quite young. There had been a car accident. His father—also in the car—survived. He was a violent drunk and became the reason that at the age of eight Mr. James ran away.

"We lived in a big, sprawling council estate, and there was an old air-raid shelter. I moved in there for a while. I can't remember when I started to tell lies and to steal. My first burglary was a sweets store. I'm not even sure what my thought process was other than I wanted sweets and I didn't have the money. After that, I started stealing the bikes in sheds."

I ASKED IF, once he started to steal, it got easier for him.

"I knew it was wrong to steal, but I wasn't sure why, other than understanding that the things I was stealing didn't belong to me."

When I told him that hadn't really answered my question, his faded blue eyes flashed irritation.

"Okay, yes," he said reluctantly. "Once I started to steal, it felt like that's what I did. I was a thief."

At the beginning, he had a smash-and-grab approach to stealing. Then he began to tag along with older boys who were breaking into bowling alleys and television stores. By the time he was eleven, Mr. James had been through the court system and was convicted of theft.

"They put me in a boys' home. There were a few orphans and a kid with severe learning disabilities, but the majority were kids like me. They'd been on the streets and had been picked up for petty thieving."

He was released at fifteen and drifted from one thing to the next, often living in abandoned buildings.

—

"MY LIFE HAD the trajectory of a pinball. It was totally reactive. I'd break into a car to sleep in it that night. I wanted to live in a house, to have a job, to be responsible, but I didn't know how to do any of those things. When I walked down the street and looked into house windows and I'd see people inside, I'd wonder, 'How do I get to be someone like that? How do I get to be a person with a purpose, a direction, a meaning, relationships, and friends? I was desperate to be a part of something, but I didn't understand the mechanisms. I knew how to weld a little bit when I was in a short-term prison sentence in my teens, I learned how—not very well, but I could weld cell doors. And afterward, I sometimes got jobs as a welder. At one point, I was working in a factory welding during the day, and as a washer in a restaurant at night, sleeping in the potato shed in the back. I read in the paper about a job course to go abroad and weld pipelines. I thought, 'That's what I need, a skill.' So I applied for a passport and got that, but I wasn't a good enough welder to pass the test for the course. If I had passed that test, it would have changed the whole course of my life," he muttered, more to himself than to me.

He pressed his lips together to stifle a sigh, and then went on.

"After that, I didn't really have a place to live, and so I became a squatter. I had no plans. In fact, the only time I remember planning anything were the petty crimes I committed. To steal parking meter heads meant that I had to first break into a hardware store to steal a pipe cutter in order to smash the heads off meters, and then I had to steal a van to take the meter heads back to the squat to break them open. They were such pathetic crimes. It went from there to these horrendous murders."

The two murders were committed three months apart and with an accomplice of whom he knew very little.

"We had nothing in common but our massive failings."

His unsparing honesty deserved acknowledging, but what it revealed did not diminish the fact that Mr. James and his co-accused were responsible for merciless murders: one victim was strangled to death in his apartment, and then, three months later, another was bludgeoned on the street.

At the age of twenty-four, Mr. James extinguished the lives of two people and forced their families into an echo chamber of anguish for the rest of theirs. Now, over three decades later, my question of whether he killed the men for money was the last thing I expected would catch him off guard. As soon as I spoke it, the molecules in the air changed, and there was a forbidding silence. I glanced down to the recording machine to make sure that the red light was still on. When I looked up, it was into an angry stare.

"That's a hell of a question," he said coldly.

It wasn't fear but bewilderment and resentment that flushed my face before I collected my wits.

"I have no idea what you might consider off-limits, but this isn't going to work for me unless I can be direct," I said to him.

I reached over to refill his cup of tea. The gesture was free enough from indictment for him to decide to answer the question.

"He wasn't meant to be in the house. I don't really want to talk about it."

Mr. James glared at me for a moment before deciding that he would.

"It was as though I couldn't get out of the circumstances and just went along with them."

"What were the circumstances of the second murder?"

"My co-accuser jumped this man. It wasn't premeditated. We were both drunk. I joined in. This poor man was beaten terribly."

Not "I beat him," but he "was beaten."

What Mr. James didn't say was that the man died four days later when his parents made the wrenching decision to turn off his life support.

I cannot imagine how Mr. James did what he did, not because of sanctimony, but because it doesn't matter what you call it, call it morality if you'd like, but it's the thing that comes between impulse and action. It's you saying to yourself, *I can't do that; I mustn't do that.*

I SAID AS much.

"Sitting with you as I am now, it's impossible for me to imagine you doing what you did."

"Even now, I can't imagine that I did what I did, but I know I did it" is how he put it. "There is nothing redeeming to my crimes. They were just horrific events, which I will never, ever be able to explain. If you asked me, 'Why did you do that?' even with the help of psychology, I can't answer."

"So, it was senseless."

"Yes," Mr. James said, through his clenched jaw.

"And you managed to escape."

"I had a passport from the time I applied for the welding program and just enough money to cross the channel to France and escape."

It was the preamble to a story that could cheat fiction; no novelist could have competed with what had really happened to Mr. James.

THE FOREIGN LEGION is a branch of the French army whose unique ordinance allows enlisted foreign nationals to fight for the French outside France. Established by King Louis-Philippe in 1831 with troops formed from disbanded Swiss and German regiments of the Bourbon monarchy, the first legionnaires landed in Algeria, which remained the legion's homeland for the next 130 years. About a quarter of the recruits are French; the rest come from some 140 other countries, making it the only unit that swears allegiance not to the country but to itself.

On the run from murdering two people in the U.K., Mr.

James joined the Foreign Legion. It appropriated his passport and accepted him without asking a single question.

Mr. James would not have been the first fugitive to join the Foreign Legion, which allows a recruit to assume a new identity. From what I understand, if any one of them is injured during a battle for France, he can apply for French citizenship under a provision, the translation of which is "French by spilled blood."

Training is physically and psychologically intense, with esprit de corps molding the men into a single culture, loyal to itself. One of its mottoes is "Legio patria nostra" (from Latin: "The legion is our fatherland"). "Honneur et fidélité" is another, which Mr. James says is what gave his life structure and morals.

He nodded appreciatively when I told him that honor, reverence, loyalty, and gallantry were the moral tenets of the chivalric code of conduct developed in the medieval late twelfth century and kept alive in the servitude of itself.

"The legionnaires are brave, they're strong, they have a code of conduct," said Mr. James, who explained that in the legion he developed scruples, which formed his character.

"Was it character that provided you with a moral consciousness?" I ask.

"Yes and no" was his answer. "There was part of me that knew I was acting. But there also came a point that I wasn't acting, because my understanding of morality had grown. When I was on night patrol in N'Djamena in Africa, I felt like a phony and a fraud. I told myself, *Here I am policing, and I should be in jail.*"

After a four-month stint in Africa, Mr. James was sent to Corsica.

"My dad came to visit me there and turned up drunk."

I asked how his father could afford to take such a trip.

"He was on benefits, but he had a part-time driving job."

"That makes perfect sense," I suggested sarcastically. "Because, I mean, as a drunk, that's exactly where he belonged—behind the wheel of a car."

Suspended between us, lasting a brief moment, appeared something neither of us expected—humor. A smile flicked near the corners of his mouth.

"I have the same name as my father," he explained. "It happened that while my father was visiting me, my co-accuser was arrested. Pleading his case, he gave them my name, and they thought it was me when my father arrived at Gatwick Airport. When I phoned him to see if he got home safely, he told me, 'You're wanted for murder.' I remember putting the phone down, thinking that the right thing to do is to go back and give myself up."

"You must have considered the consequences of handing yourself over," I said.

"Not right away. That night, I quit the Foreign Legion and walked to Calvi. The following day, I bought civilian clothes and took the ferry from Ajaccio to Nice. That's when I started to get anxious about what I was doing. I stayed on the beach for two or three nights and considered what I'd face by going back."

It was not willpower but logistics that challenged Mr. James to stick to his decision. According to Mr. James, when he arrived at the British consulate in Nice to give himself up, an elderly gentleman answered and, after being made aware of Mr. James's intention, promptly closed the door in his face.

"ARE YOU TELLING me that when you tried to give yourself up, you couldn't?"

"Not in Nice. So I started hitchhiking down the Riviera, thinking I'd go to the consul general in Marseilles. It was a hundred miles from where I was. That night I slept in a barn. The next morning I waited on the side of the road. It happened that a gendarme drove by in a jeep and I flagged him down. I was put in French prison for three months before the detectives from London brought me back to stand trial for the two murders."

"Under the circumstances, you could have disappeared and never be heard of again," I pointed out.

"When I was living a violent life, I never thought about the choices I was making," said Mr. James. "I might have had a moral capacity, but I didn't have the courage or character. It wasn't until I was in the Foreign Legion that I began to understand what morals were."

He stopped to gather his thoughts.

"What I'm trying to say is that as I grew in moral understanding, I began to understand what I had done."

It was a fully voiced declaration. Mr. James had shown character when he decided to turn himself in and then, again, when he accepted the consequences of that decision.

"I didn't feel admirable," he said, not expecting me to disagree.

"Admirable" is a word no one would allow, given the horrendous crimes for which he was responsible. In the U.K., if you don't mean to harm someone, but he or she dies, it's murder, not manslaughter. Mr. James was convicted of murder and spent twenty-three years in prison. He is still a prisoner.

"I'm on license for the rest of my life. For the first year in prison, I was locked in a cell for twenty-three hours a day with nothing more than a bed, a table, a chair, and a bucket," he said. "But I was allowed six books a week from the library. And the psychologist would give me more. She gave me *Crime and Punishment* by Dostoyevsky and Solzhenitsyn's *Cancer Ward*. It was in prison that I became a thinking reader. And it was in prison that I thought long and hard about what I had done."

Mr. James spoke of his profound guilt. "That's as it should be," he told me.

I didn't respond.

"I'm doing the best I can," he said, describing it in carefully chosen words as a prolonged battle. "I give talks in schools. It's a way of contributing, and telling my story helps me live with it."

I DOUBT I will ever see Mr. James again, but as I listened to his story, my judgment of him felt less and less the point. What took its place was an understanding of redemption, not as a mechanical thing, but as a state of extreme sorrow that led him to a committed change of life.

"You must be reading a great deal about morality since you plan to write a book about it," said Mr. James.

"Not yet," I replied.

He was hoping for more of an answer, and so I told him that for what it was worth, I thought that human beings are not intrinsically moral or immoral and that being one or the other depends on our decisions and actions. I suggested to him that one's life consists of many truths—some declaring themselves with reprehensible acts and others revealing themselves with unimagined courage.

Enough having been said, I walked Mr. James to the door.

I do not believe, ever, I will feel as conflicted as I did then, knowing that the hand he offered me to shake good-bye had strangled a person and had bludgeoned another.

Character doesn't alter with changing circumstances, and there should be no surprise when a murderer murders more than once: of these things I was sure because I grew up believing them to be true. But if there are various truths to a single life, one of Mr. James's truths—that he was a convicted murderer—made it difficult for me to acknowledge another truth: that he had become a moral being.

Somehow—against the odds—Erwin James forged a moral path out of hopelessness. It led him away from a point of no return. Uneducated, socially unsupported, given up on, possessing no skills or obvious abilities—none of this justifies the murders Erwin James committed. Nonetheless, character appeared later in his life to prove it mattered.

That is what I told him as he reached out his hand, and I shook it.

A NEUROSCIENTIST EXPLAINS THE EVOLUTIONARY ORIGINS OF MORALITY

Just remember that we are talking monkeys on an
organic spaceship flying through the universe.

—*Joe Rogan*

My library membership has been approved.

The welcome package includes a letter from the playwright Tom Stoppard. In his role as the library's current president, he sends me as many warm wishes as an Englishman offers to someone with whom he has not gone to school or does not personally know.

I return to St. James's Square confident of possessing the bibliophilic wherewithal to educate myself on the definition of morality. Crossing the library's threshold, I realize that there was far more than met the eye when I was standing in front of the building several weeks before.

Behind the limestone facade is an interior that pushes out beyond the building's width and raises several more floors than are visible from the street. Catacombs of periodicals snake belowground. Aboveground, floors disappear and reappear on different levels in a hodgepodge of connecting buildings reaching back, forward, and sideways. Inexplicably, stairways don't always have the same number of steps between contiguous floors. Cloaked in darkness are signs indicating locations of the light switches. With the exception of the main entrance and common rooms, areas of the library doze in darkness, roused occasionally by gray-toned fluorescent light when a switch is found. Warrens of floor-to-ceiling-high bookcases press in like a carpenter's vise, creating the narrowest of lanes.

According to the information in my welcome package, one of the library's basic principles is that "no book should be discarded, regardless of how idiosyncratic or unfashionable," and so, lounging comfortably in a state of benign neglect, are century-old publications. The air is stale and moldy, particularly in a section designated "Genealogy and Heraldry."

The library houses over two million volumes covering some twenty thousand subjects. A member of the staff offers to teach me to navigate the vast collections. He is astonishingly efficient, of indistinguishable age, and smells like damp tweed. The still expression on his face conveys a great deal of judgment, while the seriousness that surrounds him guards a deadpan delivery.

"Forgive me," he ventures. "But your shoes might present a problem."

The man and I are now looking down at my shoes, which—for reasons known only to him—are deemed an issue.

"Allow me to show you the library's back stacks before we tackle its catalog system," he suggests.

We climb the main stairs to the second floor, then, willy-nilly, make several sharp turns and cross into another building. Here, towering book stacks sat not on solid floors but on iron lattices whose perforated walkways permit illumination to waft unencumbered from available light sources below or above. I stand at the doorway, a safe distance from menacing floor grids that would snap the high heels I have on, as if breaking off brittle twigs.

"I take your point about the shoes," I tell the man.

He leads me back to the place from which we started, using a different, confusing route. When I mention this, his advice is otherworldly.

"Until you learn your way around, it might be easier to decide to be lost."

I cannot afford to get lost quite yet, and so I continue to trail closely behind him until he returns me to the ground floor and the welcoming glow of computer terminals where I learn about the catalog system.

The next day—wearing flat shoes and armed with a purse-size flashlight to improve my chances of locating available light switches—I return to the library fully prepared and with high hopes. Mindful of the library's classification system, and in possession of a PIN that would allow me to log on to the online catalog, I head toward the computers all too aware of my limitations with them, for in matters of technology my mind doesn't so much race ahead as lurch forward in erratic spurts. Utilizing the feature that allows me to search under the subject of my interest, I type in the word "morality."

As I scan the titles that appear on the screen, my eyes are drawn to one that includes the word "filth." An old-fashioned word with very little contemporary currency, it becomes the reason for my inaugural trip to the stacks.

Ban This Filth! is located in the psychology section, not under the author's name, but shelved alphabetically by its subject, a certain Mary Whitehouse. The black-clothed book looks like sobriety itself until I flip to its photo section, where, pictured among the great and the good, is Mrs. Mary Whitehouse, a parody of dated housewifery: prim, of a certain age, wearing a sensible skirt and plain blouse buttoned to the neck. Her hair is lacquered in place; stiffly sculptured, evenly spaced curls frame a pleasant but unremarkable face. But there is something about Mrs. Whitehouse that cannot be ignored. Beaming out from behind her cat-eye-shaped glasses is willpower that I imagine could slice through steel. I come to the only conclusion possible: in her time, Mary Whitehouse was no laughing matter.

Her time was the 1960s and 1970s, pivotal decades in the U.K., made rebellious by a new generation of bold and impatient writers, film directors, and musicians, all standing in opposition to authority. Stanley Kubrick's *Clockwork Orange* was as popular as *The Sound of Music* had been for the parents of those streaming into the movie theaters, until a media storm called for the movie to be banned. David Bowie, a bisexual art student from the multiethnic, working-class community of Brixton in south London, was reinventing himself as the flamboyantly androgynous Ziggy Stardust. It was in this cultural turbulence, pitting the young against the old, that Mrs. Whitehouse materialized—seemingly out of nowhere—determined to bring her disorderly nation to heel.

Middle age usually drains away the energy required to defend what were once our tightly held principles. That doesn't seem to be the case with religious converts, whose freshly acquired convictions lead them to new and deep reservoirs of resolve. Mary Whitehouse was a fifty-three-year-old born-again Christian schoolteacher. Possessing tireless determination and the unshakable conviction that the sanctity of all that mattered was imperiled, she launched public campaigns to stamp out what she insisted was dangerously injurious to British morality: permissiveness.

MRS. WHITEHOUSE MIGHT have been a running joke to the younger generation, but to people her age she offered an outlet for a concerned expression that their mainstream values were under assault. The enlistees in her war against what she considered immorality were parents, earners, and consumers. Their collective numbers, once organized, threatened to sway elections, which is how the improbable Mrs. Whitehouse was able to influence policy decisions within the government as well as to invoke testicle-shrinking fear among playwrights, press barons, book publishers, clergymen, and broadcasters.

A letter to Lord Hill of Luton, the then chairman of the BBC, is my favorite among her countless interventions and is dated June 16, 1972:

Dear Lord Hill,

I understand that the new Rolling Stones record, "Exile on Main Street" is being played on Radio 1.

This record uses four-letter words. Although they are somewhat blurred, there is no question about what they are meant to be.

I feel sure you will understand the concern felt about this matter, for it is surely no function of the BBC to transmit language which, as shown in a recent court case, is still classified as obscene. The very fact that this programme is transmitted primarily for young people would, one would have thought, have demanded more, not less, care about what is transmitted.

We would be grateful if you would look into this matter. Yours sincerely,
(Mrs.) Mary Whitehouse

Lord Hill's reply . . .

Dear Mrs. Whitehouse,

Thank you for your letter of June 16th in which you state that the tracks from the Rolling Stones record "Exile on Main Street," played on Radio 1 use four-letter words.

I have this morning listened with great care to the tracks we have played on Radio 1. I have listened to them at a fast rate, at a medium rate, at a slow rate. Though my hearing is excellent, I did not hear any offending four-letter words.

Could it be that, believing offending words to be there and zealous to discover them, you imagine that you heard what you did not hear?
Yours sincerely,
Ally Luton (Lord Hill)

By no means was this the first time Mary Whitehouse had been informed that she was barking up the wrong tree. That made no difference. She was determined to patrol the entire forest. Her antipornography campaign refused to be ignored, regardless of how she—or it—was handled by individuals and institutions under its attack. Mary Whitehouse gained a moral foothold and then lost it to the passage of time.

Morality changes when a way of thinking disappears, along with the vocabulary expressing it. I've seen this happen while raising my son. Never have I heard him utter the word "filth," which I use when I deem it appropriate. And when made extremely upset by something or someone, I call forth from my aging army of disapproving adjectives an even more obscure word: "vile."

Words matter, even short ones, and words you think should be the same often are not. "Mores," "morals," and "ethics" do not have the same definition; in fact, each is capable of contradicting the other two.

Introduced into the English language in the late nineteenth century by an American sociologist, the word "mores," in both its evaluative and its descriptive functions, is an assertion of the characteristic practices, conventions, and customs of a culture or society, which affect how people act.

Middle East mores dictate the custom that women cover themselves. In Dubai, no woman is penalized for not doing so, while in Saudi Arabia she might lose her life if she refuses to. Thus, mores considered no more than a custom in one country could be a deadly serious practice in another.

The English word "morality" is derived from the Latin *mores,* as is the English adjective "moral." The Greek equivalent is *ethos* and is the basis of the term "ethics." Morality is a personal set of beliefs. Ethics is expressed in the expectations and sanctions defined and enforced by a given culture or society. Frequently, ethics and morality come into total contradiction. Here's where complications ensue. A lawyer's ethical obligation is to defend to the best of his or her ability a client, even though what that person has done offends the lawyer's own moral sense. A doctor's morality may dictate that quality of life is of the utmost importance and that people should be able to select when they should die, but medical ethics might not allow the doctor to act on that moral premise.

Contrary to my self-affirming expectations of morality, it refuses to provide me with the satisfaction of universally agreed-upon ideals. Nor, it happens, do ethics, which are dictated and adjusted by a given society at a particular period of time. An important nuance in its meaning resides in "a given society at a particular period of time." That qualifier—as subtle as it is—moves ethics from any fixed point and denies its meaning a universal truth. While Middle Eastern and Asian countries censor certain musical lyrics and outlaw pornography, for example, most countries in the West hold to the principle that prohibiting both in the name of protecting moral standards infringes on free expression. Thus, one person's free expression granted by his or her society might be degradation in another. I am a distinct person with my own beliefs, one of which is that hard-core pornography demeans and is therefore wrong. But that belief amounts to no more than a personal expression of something I think wrong. Watching adult pornography—or participating in the making of it—does not hurt people. Stealing and lying do. They are wrong, irrespective of what I might think or do about them. Vexing as I find it, my personal views are secondary to protecting the cohesion within the sociocultural system in which I live and where things have certain meanings. I may not like those meanings—I may not agree with them—but I am answerable to them. Though there are alternative sociocultural systems wherein the meanings in my own cultural system do not apply, prohibitions are almost always levied against murder, theft, trespass, and false witness. And while it can be accurately said that most societies recognize the antisocial aspects of sex gone wild, eliminating permissiveness will never have the morally confident mandate of the major four ethical no-no's, so I have to quit Mary Whitehouse, as amusing and interesting as she is, and address myself to the other books on the same library shelf.

Shimmying down the aisles with my head cocked to one side in order to read the book spines, I come to a full stop at H. L. Mencken's *Treatise on Right and Wrong*. Mencken is an American, and as a fellow countryman in a foreign land I am not unsympathetic. Wiggling the book from its tightly gripped space, I flip open the cover and see that according to the date of its issue slip the last time the book has been out of the building was thirty years ago. A nagging sense of patriotism convinces me that this should be the first book on morality that I check out of the London Library.

After reading Mencken's book, I try explaining his premise of natural selection to myself. It goes something like this: *Assuming that we're the result of biology, it makes sense that the genetic traits that win are the ones that have proven to work better than the others. And I get why the survival of an individual depends not only on his honed skills but also on those of the group. Okay. Now what?*

Two blocks from my London flat is Daunt Books, one of the last in a dying breed of independent bookstores. Its narrow and winding staircases, creaky floors, and wooden counters remind me of the one in *Funny Face* where Fred Astaire discovers Audrey Hepburn. I leave with a book, recently published and recommended by Simon: Edward O. Wilson's *Meaning of Human Existence*.

According to Wilson, "Within groups selfish individuals beat altruistic individuals, but groups of altruists beat groups of selfish individuals." Wilson's theory of moral evolution is controversial by suggesting that "individual selection promoted sin, while group selection promoted virtue."

I drink *pu'er*, a strong Chinese tea, to stay awake so that I can finish the book. Because of this, I thrash about in bed at two o'clock in the morning, and while waging a battle for sleep,

I recall how my son, Gilliam—as a relatively well-mannered five-year-old—decided to embark on a brazen pursuit of immorality. In the duration of what was to him an absolutely thrilling thirty minutes, he stole money from his aunt's bureau, lied to his father about it, and turned on his grandmother—an innocent bystander during the wanton crime spree. So maniacal was the boy's behavior—so dexterous was its execution—that I became convinced a sudden biochemical alteration had turned him into a sociopath.

Almost as disturbing as Gilliam's morality-free behavior was his blasé detachment upon being told he was to answer to it by spending the rest of the day in solitary confinement. He accepted the punishment without remorse or argument and retreated to his room, where, at midday, his father decided to pay him a visit.

"What were you thinking?" asked his father.

"I wasn't thinking. I just wanted to see what it would be like" was how Gilliam explained it.

"What *what* was like?"

"To do anything I want, even if it's bad," said he.

And who would blame the boy? Few of us would turn down a debauched opportunity to do exactly what we wish. Preventing that from happening is not necessarily our moral beliefs but, more likely, the impracticality of hedonism. We are social animals, and without cooperation among us there is chaos. With the perils of chaos come distrust and disorder.

Wilson and Mencken (who defined conscience as "the inner voice which warns us that someone may be looking") agree that morality is more a matter of prudence than aspiration and that humans have little choice but to develop cohesive societies in order to survive.

So is morality in opposition to self-interest? Or is it that the well behaved reap social benefits, and thus there are more self-interested reasons than not to be moral?

I return to the library for a better understanding.

—

"THE BOOKS YOU'RE looking for will be located on the fourth floor under 'Science and Miscellaneous,'" I'm told by the same patient man who warned me about my shoes and instructed me on the computerized catalog system. "You can take the stairway," he says, pointing the way.

Nowhere is there more demonstration of the word "miscellaneous" than is found on the signs posted at the beginning of each alphabetized stack in the "Science and Miscellaneous" section of the library. The *E*s run the gamut from "Elephants" to "Estate Management"; the *H*s feature "Horseshoeing" and "Human Sacrifice." Back stairs bring me to the next floor and to banks of books in countless languages on Darwin and his theories. I choose one to read for the rest of the day, and what becomes clear to me is that from a genetic perspective and on a cellular level we are essentially selfish.

I would have preferred something nobler, but, all right, assuming that from an evolutionary point of view it's hard to be good, how do we negotiate living with one another?

Dr. Robert Trivers, an American evolutionary biologist, insists that he has the answer. Dr. Trivers is one of several pioneers of the "selfish gene" theory, which suggests that humans are unalterably in the pursuit of self-interest. Along with a British naturalist, Bill Hamilton, he would have us believe their theory of "reciprocal altruism," wherein our ability to get along with fellow humans is motivated by selfish expectations of returned favors, rather than a genuine concern for the well-being of others. If I were to use one word to describe my reaction to Mr. Hamilton's findings, I'd be torn between "despair" and "glum." I'm hoping that Molly Crockett can debunk his killjoy theory and restore my faith in humankind.

Dr. Molly Crockett has a degree in neuroscience from UCLA and another, in experimental psychology, from Cambridge. Having cut her teeth on economics at the University of

Zurich, she oversees a research lab at Oxford University exploring human decision making.

I'm not sure what I expected her to look like, but when Dr. Crockett shows up at my apartment for Sunday breakfast, she isn't it. In her thirties, appearing considerably less so, she is in possession of long black tresses, a dead serious mind, frank clear blue eyes, vibrant confidence, and an infectious smile.

Requiring Dr. Crockett to talk while she's eating would be rude, so I take the opportunity to express my bitter disappointment in the premise behind Dr. Robert Trivers's theory of reciprocal altruism. Only when Dr. Crockett has finished her meal do I ask her for her own definition of morality.

"SUCH A SIMPLE question, and such a complicated one," she says, sounding unfazed by its enormity. "For me, it starts with how you treat other people. I'm interested in why we treat others kindly. Our research suggests we are kind not only because we genuinely care about others but also because we care about our own reputation. This can lead us to cultivate a misperception of being morally better than we actually are."

Even if we're wired to cultivate that misperception, what's the point of convincing yourself that you're morally better than you actually are? Why bother?

"From an evolutionary perspective, if you can convince everyone you're trustworthy, you'll reap social benefits. The best way to do that is to believe it yourself. I'm studying how people convince themselves that they're good while behaving badly."

The vivacious Dr. Crockett has somehow managed to smile her way through a fairly unpromising premise. Confronted with such a spring-heeled take on morality from someone who knows the worst of mankind makes me think that I've missed an important point, so Dr. Crockett agrees to see me again.

For this, I must take a train to Oxford University, an ivied, encrusted, embossed, cobblestoned place where everything has played some part in history. I am to meet Dr. Crockett at Jesus College, whose 1571 charter states its intention as a college of learning in the sciences of philosophy and the moral arts.

A man in the Porters' Lodge confirms that Dr. Crockett is expecting me. He leads me across a perfectly manicured lawn toward another building and into a small common room whose paneled walls have been waxed for hundreds of years to the color of worn leather.

Seating in what feels like a giant, Jacobean humidor—interrupted by the timed intervals of tower chimes—Dr. Crockett and I have a second go at the origin of morality. I begin by pointing out the irony that our moral aspirations make us prone to subterfuge.

"Yes," says she, unconcerned.

Dr. Crockett doesn't have the jaded demeanor of the over-educated, and because she appears incapable of cynicism, I must assume that her research, not her temperament, has led her to agree with evolutionary biologists that humankind benefits from its universally dispensed half-truths. But I feel I should remind Dr. Crockett that defining a lie is not always easy: What about a half lie, or a lie that turns out to be true? I ask her. Unimpressed with my subdivision, she tells me a lie is a lie.

I can't say it's very uplifting, but I get it; we lie.

THROUGHOUT THE AGES, we have become increasingly adroit at lying. In fact, so skilled are we in deceiving one another we are likely to deceive ourselves into believing we are not hypocrites. It's not a flattering reflection of humanity, but given what Nature required of ancient man, it's one I might have guessed.

—

LIVING IN CITIES nature remained a secondary event, until the earth below me cracked like a piecrust, everything within my reach convulsed, and the world as I knew it was out of human control.

Having experienced firsthand the terror and devastation of L.A.'s Northridge earthquake, I understand why the ancients worshipped the forces of nature on which their very lives depended. I understand why, at the point man became more sophisticated, Nature alone ceased to merit worshipping. I understand why man invented gods. Imponderable to me are the reasons man invented tyrannical gods that required man to suffer. Think about it for a moment: What possible moral good did humans believe would come from introducing their gods to a taste for human sacrifice? Whose ambition did it serve?

If we were to contemplate the question of cui bono (who benefits?) in ways Darwinian, we might conclude that the grisly practice of human sacrifice was instigated by those more resourceful and clever than the rest who realized that it was an effective tool of enforcement: a ruthless king or tyrant, perhaps, who claimed that his sanctified authority was divinely ordained.

Scientists from New Zealand have established a link between human sacrifice and the more socially stratified societies, leading them to believe that the practice of human sacrifice legitimized class-based power and, conversely, that the more egalitarian the society, the less likely it practiced human sacrifice.

If we were to accept that among our forebearers the key to a person's power was to appear as if he had a hotline to the gods, does it mean that whoever the divine leader happened to be in any particular tribe or society, what he decreed as right and good became the mores of that tribe or society? And if that were so, might it then mean that what we call ethics began as the agendas of those in control and the concept of moral values was really power in disguise?

4

A BRIEF HISTORY OF MANKIND'S ATTEMPTS TO REIN IN BAD BEHAVIOR

On the whole, human beings want to be good,
but not too good, and not quite all the time.

—*George Orwell*

Even if we put aside the conjecture that morality was a Machiavellian contrivance, it still should not come as a surprise that mortals eventually rejected sacrificial rituals demanded by their pagan gods, whose purpose was to strike abject fear into the masses. No surprise either when, finally—after years of being forced to work above their pay grade for tolerance—mortals decided that they had had enough from their Greek and Roman gods who, when not punishing them, were capriciously toying with them.

Humankind recognized the value of safety in numbers and devised a system of worship that diversified the deities. What had been a relatively small number of gods was replaced with a multitude of local cults. Morality became decentralized: every village had its own god, each god its own priest, and each priest placed his own stamp on interpreting divine decrees.

WITH PRIESTS VYING for power outside their fiefdoms, Amenhotep, Egyptian pharaoh of the eighteenth dynasty (whose chief consort was Nefertiti and whose son was Tutankhamen), came to believe that the disparateness of the gods and their squabbling priests would likely divide his people and that a divided people would plague his government. Reasoning that a great empire required one, galvanizing god, Amenhotep banished the local divinities and ordained that his people worship a single supreme force: Aten, the sun god. The afterlife was assigned to Osiris.

Holding a crook in one hand and a flail in the other, Osiris cut quite a figure, despite his mummified legs. The single feathers on either end of his Mardi Gras crown served a purpose. The deceased's heart was weighed against one of the two feathers. If it was lighter than the feather, the deceased was allowed to keep his heart and granted passage to paradise. Heavier, not good: a demonic crocodile would eat the deceased's heart, leaving him to wander forever in a soulless place that was neither paradise nor earth.

No one can argue that demonic crocodiles are an effective scare tactic for the living to behave, but the point worth considering here is that by 1550 B.C. Egyptians believed in a divine judgment and the nature of man's moral behavior had been determined.

ONCE HIS REIGN ended, Amenhotep's single-god strategy was replaced with a pantheon of gods reclaiming moral authority, but by now the rules were less absolute and the rituals not as compelling. One thing led to another . . .

Greek thinkers proposed that moral responsibility be placed squarely on man's shoulders.

Fair warnings came from Sophocles's plays reiterating what a mistake it is to expect fairness from fellow humans.

Determined to pin down the metaphorical location of morality, Pythagoras suggested that there was a correlation between mathematics and the harmonious proportions constituting moral behavior—that the *mean* was a fixed midway between two extremes, and that moral behavior was, therefore, the *mean* between one's behavioral extremes.

While it is true that no religion can boast of an unsullied history, all religions are clear on designating moral convictions. Founded by the Iranian prophet Zarathustra in the fifth century B.C., Zoroastrianism, possibly the oldest religion, rests on three principles: have good thoughts; say good words; do good deeds. Hinduism, another ancient religion, prescribes the moral duties of honesty and self-restraint, regardless of class, caste, or sect. Confucius, born 551 years before Christ, wrote, "Aspire to the principle, behave with virtue, abide by benevolence."

If you have any doubt that the East found a higher angle for metaphysical perspective than did the West, you need only compare the profundity in the sixth-century B.C. scriptures of Taoism with some of the unhinged instructions found in the Old Testament.

Christianity, a relative newcomer, might have remained a regional phenomenon had it not been for imperial trade routes enabling its teachings a passage into the Roman Empire. More a policy decision than a religious awakening, the Roman emperor Constantine declared Christianity the official religion of the Roman Empire. He turned religion into power by pouring money into the church; promoting Christians to higher offices; and sanctioning the premise of Moses's Ten Commandments, which established an indestructible grounding for moral behavior in the West.

There was nothing novel about prohibitions of murder, theft, trespass, and adultery; these were already recognized in virtually every other society, and their ideas overlapped Eastern canons. What was strikingly new about the commandments was what was etched at the top of their stone tablet: "I, Yahweh, am thy God" and "Thou shalt have no other gods."

—

BECAUSE I AM, by nature, wary of any institution claiming to possess a truth unavailable to the rest of us unless we join its rank and file, I am especially alert to the first two of the Ten Commandments. They seem to me to convey a message devoid of spiritual generosity. Allow me also the liberty of suggesting that most religions have revealed grievous disparities between what might initially have been commendable moral strategies and the often reprehensible practices employed to implement them.

In this far, I might as well say it: never are religions more convinced of their own version of the moral truth as when they pronounce something incredible. Limbo as the destination of souls of unbaptized babies, for instance, was once an unwavering truth issued by the church. It was recently retired as a concept, but only after the imposition of it caused untold unhappiness for generations among those dutiful believers who were parents of such babies. It is this type of conceptual U-turn that forces me to question whether religion is the source of morality or simply a thought system that doesn't always lead to compassionate decisions.

Having repeatedly proven that there is no intellectual dead end too futile for it to pursue, the church—enabled by the concept of sin—prevented advancement by various methods, the most decisive of which was to burn scientists, writers, and philosophers at the stake and to destroy their work.

That I am more a believer in my own self-reflective consciousness than in a specific god doesn't prevent me from acknowledging religion's considerable powers of moral repair. Humankind is in need of all the help it can get, because, let's face it, when left to our conscience, the results are often disappointing.

Fortunately, during what must have been an outbreak of common sense in the fourth century, a Greek monk came to the sound conclusion that explicit rules were required to hold man to account. Evagrius Ponticus set about organizing a punch list of temptations from which springs all sinful behavior. Ignoring any one of the temptations was a failure to do what was morally required.

Two hundred years later, Pope Gregory identified these same temptations concisely in single words. Plainly numbered, the seven deadly sins became shorthand to what is more aspirational than applicable morality, for who among us has not partaken in at least one of the deadly sins? Some of our politicians have trafficked in all seven: after all, greed, pride, envy, wrath, sloth, lust, and a bit of gluttony are the currencies of power.

Pride is a kind of marquee sin. To indulge in it requires overconfidence, which is the first step on the ruinous path to hubris, or so it has been foretold as far back as the Greek gods, with their doom-laden warnings. I remain dubious that pride is a destructive force, for I have lived among those whose immodest self-regard has passed the test of time—the French.

If you've attempted to make a home among the French, as I have, no doubt you noticed that they refuse to admit they might not know something. The best you'll get is conveyed in deflective past tense, *Je ne sais plus,* "I no longer know."

It's not just the French people but also their inanimate objects that resign themselves to a shrug when there's a problem. Their fax machines, for example, flagging a failed attempt to send or receive, will signal *erreur distante,* "a distant error," more existential disclaimer than admission of a mechanical problem.

Pride among the French has a jaunty insouciance to it, as though hubris itself were wearing a jacket raffishly draped over its shoulders, leaning against a wall in the nonsmoking zone enjoying a Gauloises cigarette.

Fueling their confidence is the belief that French culture is better in all things—a claim difficult to challenge with a nation smaller than Texas that has produced Camus, Impressionist painting, mille-feuille, Erik Satie, and appreciation for runny brie, to name only a few. Indeed, countless superlatives contribute to the validity of French pride. It also helps that they are convinced that God is French.

With the exception of predominantly Catholic French (more French than Catholic), who believe the purpose of life should be the seeking of pleasure, cultures formed by religions embrace a belief that humility provides man with the opportunity to change his behavior for the better. We might aspire to a greater good and admire excellence, but in our daily lives we struggle with what is less than good or less than excellent, while our apathy vies for supremacy.

By no means do I believe that religion is a prerequisite of moral behavior (though, according to various polls, Americans believe this to be precisely the case), but it has been my experience that achieving—and, perhaps even more difficult, maintaining—admirable behavior without the benefit of religious belief calls on a great deal of personal discipline. Acknowledging oneself as an atheist or an agnostic requires a dedicated, lifelong contemplation of what is meant by right and wrong in social terms, rather than by reference to salvation or the law of God, and without the carrot of heavenly rest or the stick of hell's fire.

I hold to the belief that the way we were, and the way we are, and the way we will be are the result of the choices we make, which is why I'm intrigued when I learn about the "everyone is responsible for his or her moral self" basis of Deism, a more philosophical than theological take on morality. Its way of thinking was practiced by the ancient Greeks before gaining prominence during the eighteenth century, specifically in Europe during the Enlightenment.

One of the most influential contributors toward the Enlightenment was Jean-Jacques Rousseau. Given the opportunity these past few weeks to become more acquainted with him, I have been won over by his up-by-the-bootstraps attitude toward morality: that it doesn't come without self-denial, without struggle, and without effort. It must also be said that I'm attracted to the way he looks: portraits show an arched good nature to his eyebrows. I admire his brilliance: as a political philosopher, his works formed the cornerstones of modern social thought; as a novelist, he set in motion the idea of romanticism in fiction; as a writer of nonfiction, he initiated introspection in modern autobiography; as a composer of music, his output included several operas. I especially like Rousseau for believing that insofar as they lead people to virtue, all religions are equally worthy and that, if belief in a higher being increases the likelihood of virtue, one should allow it a say.

Richard Dawkins doesn't want to.

Dawkins is a biologist, a science writer, a broadcaster, and an author. More than any of these things, he is a militant atheist excelling in provocation. Though I am hard put to disagree with his fundamental premise—that accepting some of the more outlandish aspects of religion can be an impediment to the function of logic—I understand how people might think he's smug, because Mr. Dawkins often gives the impression that he is the only adult in the room. During one of his talks I attended in London, he suggested that believing in a higher being was, well, stupid.

Many smart people in the audience disagreed.

Understatement is a way of life among the English, and there is a certain kind of composure locked into the British that manages to escape to their language. Since living here, I've heard news reports referring to intermittent gale warnings as "unsettled weather" and disastrous political decisions described as "very unhelpful." So mannerly are the British that even when they are seething with indignation, rarely do they speak up, and if they do, what they actually mean is almost always obscured by how they express themselves. This was the case during the question-and-answer phase of Mr. Dawkins's talk. When he suggested that religion is an excuse to evade the need to think, the man to my left prefaced his objection with "with all due respect." What he really meant was "you are an idiot." And when Dawkins insisted that at times faith qualifies as a kind of mental illness, the man seated behind me suggested that Dawkins "might consider a different perspective." What this meant was "I don't like you at all."

Oscar Wilde wrote that morality is the attitude we adopt toward people whose behavior we personally dislike. The rebel in me doesn't like a sermon, and by any other name Mr. Dawkins's strident opinions organize themselves like one. Still, I don't dislike Mr. Dawkins. How can I? I don't know him. But it seems to me that (1) puzzling out what lies beyond us is what we humans do, (2) there is righteousness on both sides of what is a very personal belief in God or no God, (3) science is less at odds than religion with how it was that we came to be, and (4) this is probably the reason science is willing to accommodate a philosophical take on morality when religion hesitates to do so.

Modern-day philosophers chart moral perspectives from a system of *moral absolutism* to one of *moral relativism*. The first is based on the belief that various principles ought never to be violated; the second, that a given action does not depend solely on social custom or individual acceptance. My belief system has always resided with the former—the "that's the way it has to be" version of morality.

Truth be told, that moral approach has not brokered me any favors. Certainly not in China, whose culture resides comfortably in what the West considers moral ambiguity. The times I tried pointing out what was to me a fundamental right and wrong in business transactions (for example, the veracity of a signed contract), it was as if I were arguing with fog. The longer I remained in China, the more I feared getting lost in a shamelessness of moral relativism.

It turned out that I need not have worried as much as I did, for shame in the West has become less and less an issue, especially when it comes to matters of money.

PART TWO

Morality's Scorecard

THE EDITOR OF THE *FINANCIAL TIMES* PROVIDES A COST-BENEFIT ANALYSIS OF PRINCIPLES

He who has never cheated cannot be a good businessman.

—*Chinese proverb*

Studies I read on how we behave around money do little to build my confidence in man's moral integrity. My research confirms that the degree we feel shame changes when cash is involved and that empathy is more likely expressed if it doesn't come with financial cost.

"If I were a visitor from another planet, how would you explain money to me?" I asked Lionel Barber, the editor of the *Financial Times.*

Even though he is a very smart man able to clothe the most mundane topic of money with meaning and wit, Mr. Barber has a momentary look of befuddlement.

"Money is a medium of exchange" is how he begins. "It allows people to buy and sell goods and services. There's paper money, but there's also, if you like, virtual money where things are done on credit."

NICELY ANSWERED.
Mr. Barber has somehow managed to make restraint feel

vibrant and has refrained from embellishing his definition of money with an opinion of it. I, on the other hand, do not run one of the world's leading business and news operations, and so I suggest to him that money has a nasty tendency to awaken the least attractive qualities in human beings, many of whom are determined to invent illegal and immoral methods of acquiring it.

So pervasive is bad behavior around money we are rarely shocked by it anymore. When, for instance, it was learned that the lucrative opportunity of hosting soccer's World Cup had been corrupted within FIFA for the better part of two decades by shadowy dealings normally reserved for drug cartels, few were surprised when it was revealed that cottage industries had sprung up around that systematic corruption. Hats off, some insisted, for the enterprising man who, having helped funnel bribes among officials, charged an annual fee of $150,000, plus a 2 percent commission for each payment.

On the rare occasion we do become depressed by greed's reach into business, it's usually upon discovering that it's not a single person, not even a few people, but an entire company that has deceived the system. The public finally found its disgust when it discovered that Volkswagen, Europe's largest company, fully aware that emissions of nitrogen oxides cause early deaths, installed software on 1.1 million of its diesel cars worldwide. This enabled them to pass the emission tests in the United States, whose approval is granted only upon meeting strict anti-pollutant requirements. Once the cars left the laboratory with an approval, the software deactivated the car's emission control. VW knowingly released cars that would spew out fumes up to forty times the permitted level. The software it inserted into the cars in order to bypass environmental standards was called a "defeat device." That's right, the mechanism had a name as unapologetic as the calculating, cynical, greedy decision to install it.

Greed, one of the seven deadly sins, is insatiable: no sooner have we attained what we've convinced ourselves will satisfy us than we want more.

Greed is also one of the basic drivers of capitalism. For this reason, we impose on it regulations and fines.

So, with billions of dollars in fines and warranty costs at stake, why were the risks inherent in this kind of conspiracy so brazenly ignored—especially by Germans, with their culture-based beliefs in rigorous discipline?

The only possible conclusion I can come to is that there is no accounting for human behavior, which would explain why unethical business practices defy any one particular culture.

JAPAN'S MITSUBISHI MOTORS has also admitted that it cheated for twenty-five years on fuel economy tests with incorrectly measured fuel efficiency data. And when a group of global news organizations published articles based on leaked confidential documents from a law firm in Panama, it exposed a geographically diverse group of people with two things in common: personal wealth, and the wherewithal to conceal it in offshore bank accounts in order to avoid paying taxes. The rogues' gallery included the prime ministers of Iceland and Pakistan, the presidents of Argentina and Ukraine, the king of Saudi Arabia, the former emir of Qatar, and the relatives of several current and former members of China's ruling Politburo.

Predating by several centuries Panama's ethically questionable service to the world's rich are Swiss banks. Bank secrecy in Switzerland protected the funds brought home by mercenaries during the Middle Ages, and it has since enabled safe havens for the wealth of the most immoral among us: dictators, despots, arms dealers, and corrupt officials.

Not long ago, the banks in Switzerland represented nearly 60 percent of the total value added to that country's financial sector, so you can see how self-regulation would have been counterintuitive. Only recently has harsh criticism against the rich in the U.K. hiding their riches forced an agreement between the government and that of the Swiss regarding undisclosed bank accounts. This year the U.S. Justice Department discovered that Swiss banks were advising some of their U.S. clients to load funds onto untraceable credit cards as a method of evading taxes.

That money seems to bring out the worst in most of us—no matter our nationality—might have something to do with how humankind has organized itself, anthropologically speaking. According to Alan Fiske, an American professor of anthropology known for his work on the nature of human relationships, we've historically handled ourselves in four different and sequential systems of social interaction, with each of the four shaping its own set of moral standards, different from those preceding it.

The first of the four social models was based on communal sharing, when who was getting what didn't matter. This proposition fills me with admiration, but it also surprises me, because I've always assumed that keeping score was what humans do, especially with members of your own family.

The second model is authority based and features a hierarchy between dominant and subservient—a model made venerable by the dissatisfaction that occurs among those falling below the bottom line.

The third model is reciprocal and relies on bartering. I've done this when, docking at a remote, hutted village during a trip down the Amazon River, I traded a pocket-size sewing kit for the ten-foot-long boa constrictor snakeskin that currently hangs on the wall in my apartment. It initially belonged to a man skinning the snake for his dinner. The man and I were equally delighted by the transaction, albeit for different reasons.

The fourth model calls on currencies and finance to measure tangibles. It pins investment and trading to the economic fundamentals of cash flow, interest rates, product lineup, growth, and mergers and acquisitions. But this current model has gone through a revamp and is now able to divorce itself from the economic fundamentals. Modern technology—the kind that most of us will never understand much less have access to—enables the making of money by anticipating what the market is going to do. Superconductors implement thousands of trades a millisecond, creating and eliminating wealth in ways that have nothing to do with actual work.

When I ask Mr. Barber if he believes that there is any one way of making money more moral than another, he reminds me that after the financial crisis Lord Turner, a top regulator in the U.K., introduced the concept of socially useless banking, that is, transactions with money that created no value whatsoever.

With certain people in possession of more money than some sovereign nations, what, I ask, is the benefit of an individual's making hundreds of millions times more than he or she needs and anyone else has?

"I think it's hard to justify some of the pay levels of certain people in the world today, particularly in the West; they're so extraordinarily out of sync with others," says Mr. Barber. "The question for me is, what are they going to do with that money? If they are giving to philanthropic causes or for educational purposes, I'd welcome that, and I think the Americans have shown something of the way for other countries. That Bill Gates and Warren Buffett are pledging up to 98 percent of their personal wealth is very encouraging."

True, Gates, Buffett, and, more recently, Mark Zuckerberg—with the distribution of their vast sums of money—give moral meaning to the idea that wealth can be a good unto itself. On the other hand, Thomas Jefferson, another great American, had no quarrel with the belief that money, not morals, was the principal commerce of civilized nations, and I wonder if that is why, while we might only disdain politicians, we are likely to detest bankers. Does Mr. Barber think that leading up to the crisis, the unregulated banking system was immoral?

"In the financial sector, if you don't have a direct relationship with the risk, you're not going to be ultimately accountable . . . and that can lead to recklessness and immorality."

Mr. Barber is exercising restraint once again; what he's said is for the sake of ambiguity as much as it is intended for clarity. To his point comes mine: that individuals in the financial sector have violated ethical norms for the sake of greed. There has always been greed, but when leverage is made available, and regulations are disabled, greed grabs hold on an unimagined scale not just with individuals and institutions but with entire financial systems. Before the euro took a death march through Greece, that country joined the eurozone aware that its economy was fundamentally corrupt. During the following eight years, it borrowed billions of dollars from European banks, and all the while it was lying to EU officials about its debt. By 2010, Greece, a country of ten million inhabitants, was carrying an estimated $430 billion in debt.

Sensing that I've overextended my limited knowledge on the subject of free markets, I track back to a more general discussion by suggesting that while it is true that more people in the world are being lifted out of poverty than ever before, it is also true that during the last three decades, inequity has risen dramatically, due, in some part, by compensation increases for those in banking and business routinely associated with underperformance and at times illegality. One of the more memorable sleight-of-hand examples is the former CEO of the New York Stock Exchange, a nonprofit company, who was awarded $187.5 million as part of a go-away package when, in 2003, the market was dragging along the bottom.

"I think everything's changed as a result of the global financial crisis and the fact that banks were bailed out with taxpayers' money to the tune of billions of dollars," says Mr. Barber. "It doesn't really matter that, for example, in America the government's made that money back, people are talking about income inequality and looking at the data. The gap between what those running big businesses earn and ordinary workers earn has increased far more than even the gilded age in the

Roaring Twenties, so I think the framework of the debate has changed."

IT'S NOT DIFFICULT to see how morality can become beside the point in the institutional making, spending, and accumulation of money. According to the data compiled by Reuters, the financial sector as a whole has paid out $235 billion for breaching regulations. Moral calculation seems to have been based on how much profit can be made before someone is caught at a malfeasance and after the fine for it has been paid.

Fining a business, rather than pursuing criminal charges against the individuals responsible, allows profit to be put before moral rectitude. If there are no jail sentences—only fees—for wrongdoings, executives can calculate penalty fees into their company's profit and loss account (as they have been known to do), and what should be a moral decision becomes a financial one. Having paid the fee, they feel no guilt because there is nothing to feel guilty about.

Behaving morally is less likely to occur without rules of law that establish a fair distribution of money—not perfectly fair, but minimally fair. So where's moral debate today? I ask.

"The law has become so complicated and made it much harder to pin down the nature of a crime," explains Mr. Barber. "It's easier to, in effect, have a plea bargain."

IT SEEMS TO me that unless the capitalistic system actively works to prevent the kind of behavior that has occurred all too often in the financial sector, inaction will continue to produce profound inequities. In America, there have been only a modest number of criminal charges brought against senior bank executives, and in Britain, where burglary can mean up to fourteen years in prison, price-fixing cartels get five years at the most. The U.K. has had to bail out three of its biggest banks, and more than $100 billion have been paid since 2009 to settle claims. *One hundred billion dollars,* and yet not a single banker has gone to jail or admitted guilt. In that sense, Mr. Barber believes that morality has been lost.

We touch on how our parents' generation conducted business. My father believed that his handshake was his word and that his word was his bond. Neither of those beliefs interfered with his successful business career. Today, the context has changed, and most people don't consider a handshake to be binding. I suggest to Mr. Barber that the handshake example is a useful illustration of a reciprocal recognition within society and institutions and that when reciprocity breaks down, what were once moral expectations fall away. No longer do we expect a handshake to be a bond, and one's word is not expected to be binding.

I ask Mr. Barber if he thinks that this is true with the larger moral picture: that because of the relatively few criminal prosecutions in banking, the consensus has become to expect less of morality. "Do you think morality is the consensus of the majority?" is how I put it.

"I'm not sure it's majoritarian," he tells me. "I think it depends upon the voices in society who are capable of influencing public opinion, which then translates into statute or policy. It's interesting, for example, in Britain, the way the archbishop of Canterbury, who, in one or two earlier cases, was seen as somewhat of a peripheral figure, somewhat eccentric . . . the new archbishop of Canterbury is a former oil executive . . . a businessman. And he now is setting the terms of debate on morality in this country very effectively."

Setting the terms to debate about morality in the financial sector, and not applying criminal sanctions for abuse that has resulted in other people's loss of their life savings, are two separate things. The week after my interview with Mr. Barber, an unrepentant chief executive of one of the few banks actually prosecuted called his firm's felonious behavior "an embarrassment," as if resulting from a fleeting social faux pas. My first reaction was that the man was without shame. After giving it further thought, I realized that it wasn't that this man was unable to find the through lines between doing something wrong and feeling shameful. It was simply that he believed he'd done nothing wrong.

There wasn't always the egregious consumption and the shameless selling of integrity that have crept into contemporary culture. Granted, they were philosophers, not moneymen, but Aristotle and Confucius, living on opposite ends of the earth roughly two centuries apart, believed that the highest enterprise of man was knowledge rather than the quest for worldly goods.

We can credit the scripture in the Gospels of Matthew, Mark, and Luke that attributed to Jesus the logistically impossible but nonetheless intriguing notion that "it is easier for a camel to go through the eye of a needle than for a rich man to enter into the kingdom of God." Some three hundred years later, Cyril of Alexandria put the quotation in spatial perspective by claiming that the word *kamelos,* "camel," is a Greek misprint for the word *kamilos,* meaning "rope." Typos or no, Paul made himself unmistakably clear with his warning: "The love of money is the root of all evil."

Not until the Middle Ages, when reconciling itself to a more commercially based economic model, did European society begin to believe the making of money—that is to say, work—was a catalyst to moral virtue, proving that like so many other self-invented conceits of mankind the concept of money has not been defined by ethical consistencies. So we might do well to ask if a change in moral codes is a logical solution to the changing necessities of the times. Certainly it was the reason that during both the Middle Ages and the Renaissance moneymaking through sustained work became necessary. And why commerce in the eleventh century gave rise to the merchant, who created work for those who had been dislocated by feudal society. Perhaps it's why Martin Luther is credited for his doctrine on the dignity of work. "Vocation" and "a calling" became synonymous. Luther placed a coin in the sweaty hand of labor, and Calvin upped the ante by assigning Christian virtues to industry and enterprise.

It's since become obvious that rewarding the work ethic did very little—if anything at all—to lift mankind to a higher moral rung. And after spending several weeks being introduced to the moral pitfalls of moneymaking, I come to the woeful conclusion that humans will always do what humans have always done, including cheat when it comes to money. Adding to this downbeat note is my suspicion that bad behavior probably succeeds more often than we care to admit.

The question, then, becomes, what should be done about both of these things?

6

INSTRUCTIONS ON HOW NOT TO CHEAT

Where large sums of money are concerned,
it is advisable to trust nobody.

—*from Agatha Christie's novel* Endless Night

Four months into my search for modern morality, I am positioned in the upper reaches of British society on the first floor of London's Athenaeum Club. My guest is a former Royal Bank of Scotland banker under whose watch the interest-rate-rigging scandal began, and he has gone on the record that he will not take responsibility, insisting that he'd attempted to instill the right values in those who reported to him.

"You can't impose a moral standard on people who don't wish to be moral," he tells me, in his lead-up to recommending Jonathan Haidt's book *The Righteous Mind,* which puts across the proposition that the act of reasoning has been evolved to further our personal agendas, to justify our own actions, and to defend the so-called teams to which we belong.

THAT MIGHT BE. But there is an important distinction between morals and ethics that should be made on behalf of those who relied on the integrity of the banker and his bank. It is this: morality is what an individual believes is acceptable behavior; those in a position to dictate what should and should not be acceptable behavior promulgate ethics. There are ethics in medicine, there are professional ethics in the field of law, and—difficult to believe at times, but true—there are ethics in banking. It may well be that you can't instill morality in people who do not wish to be moral, but you can definitely hold them to ethical standards, and it seems to me reasonable to expect the CEO of a bank—along with all other senior bank and business executives—to lead.

Often it is difficult for us to act in accordance with what is a moral way of behaving without the benefit of guidelines for that, which is why leaders are called for—individuals capable of setting and maintaining moral guidelines within an organization. The good news for those extremely well-paid bank and corporate officers who seem to find that task too difficult to handle on their own is that help can be found online.

ROGER STEARE IS visiting professor of organizational ethics at City University of London's Cass Business School, who, according to the home page of his website, presents an opportunity for CEOs, board directors, and executives to learn how to think differently in order to "make right what's wrong" and to "make better what is already right." For personal use, there is a free-of-charge personality profile called MoralDNA, co-designed by Professor Steare.

HOW MORALDNA™ WORKS

We measure three decision-making preferences: the Law, Logic and Love. From the order of your preferences, we define your MoralDNA™ character— Philosopher, Judge, Angel, Teacher, Enforcer or Guardian. We also measure "Who you are" and "Who you are at work," to see if you change in a business context. Finally, we score you on the ten moral values of Wisdom, Fairness, Courage, Self Control, Trust, Hope, Humility, Care, Honesty and Excellence.

"Consider the source" is practical advice, especially when it comes to someone who offers to help you understand how you make what you believe to be the right decisions. I decide to speak to Professor Steare by phone before taking his test.

Our discussion commences in polite disagreement on whether ethics and morals are one and the same.

"THE DEFINITION OF ethics is the study of moral philosophy" is how Professor Steare begins. "So the two words can be used interchangeably. In terms of common usage, 'ethics' tends to be used in a professional context, while 'morality' tends to be used in a more citizenship context."

Bearing in mind that we've just begun our conversation, I try gently nudging Professor Steare closer to my perspective.

"In terms of morality, one is answerable to oneself and one's higher being" is how I position it. "Ethics, on the other hand, come with societal and cultural structures, albeit structures that may vary from society to society and culture to culture. Would you not agree with that?"

It seems Professor Steare would not.

"Some people might have that definition, but it's not one that I find helpful," he tells me. "What we're interested in is how people make decisions and then do the right thing, both for their own conscience and the conscience of the group to whom they are attached. I don't think you should get hung up on the two words."

IF I'M HUNG up on the two words, it's because I think they shouldn't be assigned the same meaning. It seems to me that ethics are the overt embodiment of a system of ideas, while morals are what we expect from ourselves, personally. Sensing that my point might be more effectively conveyed if I were to use an example, I refer Professor Steare to a recent news item about the owner of an American company who made the moral decision to restrict his company's paid medical insurance plan to one that didn't cover the cost of birth control.

"As an individual, the man certainly had the right to his personal, moral belief. But as the CEO of a company, he made an ethical decision that had legal implications. Under these circumstances, morals beliefs and ethics were two different things."

"I acknowledge that," concedes Professor Steare. "But a debate about the difference between ethics and morality is less important than understanding what it means to make better decisions in order to do the right thing."

Professor Steare is concerned that I am missing an important insight: that often people's morality or ethics change according to the group to which they belong.

"MORALDNA DOESN'T DESCRIBE people as moral or immoral," says he. "Every human being and group of human beings do things that are good, and they do things that are bad, and they do them both consciously and unconsciously. The question here is about intent and mindfulness. Most of us go through life making decisions by habit, rather than stopping to think about what we're doing or how we're doing it. The work I do is to slow down and stop the unthinking, inconsiderate, narrow focus of business leaders and to get them to think about why they do what they do."

An adviser to the boards and senior executives of major corporations, public sector institutions, governments, and regulators, Professor Steare operates with the belief that with few exceptions humans are born with innate ethical or moral constructs; that we are pro-social animals requires this of us. This is a different perspective on the evolutionary origins of morality than was offered to me at Oxford by Dr. Molly Crockett.

"Through a process, we can elevate thinking to a more conscious, mindful level so people make better decisions," Professor Steare tells me.

Personally, I don't think one can be trained to do the right thing for the sake of doing the right thing, but I appreciate the sanguinity on which it theoretically pivots; it's the same as being convinced before the end of the movie *Casablanca* that the amorally inclined Captain Renault, when given a chance to behave morally, would come around.

After what was for me an inconclusive phone discussion with Professor Steare, I am nonetheless prepared to take his MoralDNA test on my computer screen so that I can discover if I am to be considered a moral Philosopher, Judge, Angel, Teacher, Enforcer, or Guardian.

Among the test's series of questions are, *Do you consider yourself impulsive, compassionate, fair?* and so on, which are answered by ticking boxes. Choices of the answers range between the two goalposts of "strongly agree" and "strongly disagree." "There are no right or wrong answers," it wants you to believe.

Of course there's a right or wrong answer, I say to myself, ticking my way through the various boxes.

Moments after I complete the test, the results arrive as an e-mail:

> *Your test scores tell us that you are: Any type*
> *While you are described as a Judge, this is our best guess based on your results. Your test scores tell us that you display no distinct preference between the three ethics; the differences in scores being too small to identify you as a particular type. You could, therefore, fall into any one of the profile types.*

It's not the first time that I've been fingered as someone operating out of category, so the "any type" reference doesn't bother me. What galls me is the part that suggests that I am probably judgmental.

There's a difference between being judgmental and having correct judgment, I tell the invisible jury in my head. *I have a problem with people who cheat, lie, and are unkind. I won't apologize for that.* Thinking on the matter further forces me to admit that there might be a few more examples of my intolerance, though I am unable to recall them offhand. I ask the person who knows me best if he thinks I deserved to be put in MoralDNA's category of "Judge."

"You are the most judgmental person imagined," my son tells me.

I wasn't sure whether to be more insulted by Gilliam's overly forward manner or self-conscious by the truth it conveyed, but the look I gave him was enough to remind him of my station as his mother.

"I'm sorry," he apologized, "is there another way of putting across the point?"

I have raised Gilliam from boy to young man on my own, and making up for my ribbing of the French is the backhanded compliment that I sent him through their educational system. Also, because I have cast aspersions on the financial sector, now might be a good time to confess that it employs him. As his mother, I'm relieved to report that he has not seen jail time, though I shall refrain from speculating if this is due to his upbringing, his character, or the fact he is certifiably moral. That's right. The young man has earned a required certificate by the U.K. and the EU guaranteeing that he is a morally responsible person.

Gilliam is a China research analyst who splits his time between offices in London and Beijing, where he happens to be when I become curious about the process of his moral certification. The seven-hour time difference between us makes a phone conversation a challenge to schedule.

"Please provide details of just how you came by your certi-fication," I ask by way of an e-mail.

He writes back.

"The Financial Conduct Authority is the UK version of the US's Securities and Exchange Commission. Because it has neither the resources nor the inclination to vet individuals for their moral awareness, it outsources this task to for-profit companies that formulate multiple-choice exams. The exams allow plausible deniability for the firms should their employees behave badly."

In addition to the need to pass numerous exams for his var-ious certificates, Gilliam was expected to memorize the FCA's eleven principles for business, which include such systematic basics as "A firm must conduct its business with integrity; a firm must conduct its business with due skill, care and dili-gence; a firm must take reasonable care to organise and control its affairs responsibly and effectively, with adequate risk man-agement systems."

"Every system has a way of dealing with the inevitable inef-ficiencies of its function without throwing the system itself into question" is Gilliam's concluding e-mailed thought on the matter.

I'm not clear on the point he's making. We agree to a video call over the weekend.

Sunday afternoon London time, which is his late eve-ning, Gilliam appears on my computer screen and asks me if I know why John Nash was awarded the Nobel Prize. I do not know why John Nash received a Nobel Prize, but I am looking at my son thinking that he needs a haircut.

"Nash's work was the cornerstone in developing today's understanding of game theory."

I wait for more.

"Game theory is based on a fundamental understand-ing," he explains. "When confronted with a system, we seek to adapt to that system in order to maximize personal ben-efit while minimizing risk. To the human mind, everything is some kind of system, defined as a framework of fixed points and variables that can be manipulated in order to achieve a specific result. Families are systems. Societies are systems. Traffic is a system. Learning is a system. Biology is a system. Music is a system. Anything that has rules is a system. Systems are derived from the necessity of order. We are hardwired to create, identify, internalize, and exploit the rules of any given situation we're in."

"Okay . . ."

"Well, finance is a system that turns profit by rendering itself as efficient as possible."

"That's a rather restrictive reading."

"I think this," my son wanted to make clear, "morality is ultimately a personal choice, one that differs based on the individual and the circumstances in question. When put in a position of considering personal benefit against potential harm to others, a man will rely on his own moral compass to determine what is right, and no amount of forced memorization will change the direction in which that compass points."

I don't disagree that human nature should be the target for enforcing morality, not economic systems. But I think that it's worth recognizing the importance of creating conditions for our behavior, and I tell Gilliam that given what I've learned the past several months about the dastardly selfish gene in humans, it seems to me that institutional preconditions are the only tools by which to improve the chances of acceptable behavior and that the certificate regime required in the financial service sector is better than no regime at all.

"It's not just a question of taking an exam, passing it, and receiving a certificate," Gilliam tells me. "I'm required to have periodic reviews."

"Reviews for what purpose?" I ask.

"To ensure that I haven't forgotten how to be moral," he says.

Gilliam is expected to read case studies sent to him online.

I ask for recent examples. He sends me two. The cases are real, but the names have been changed and actors are used.

I'm not sure that a picture speaks as many as a thousand words, but I am immediately struck by the physical representation of two men paired, as they have been, with their offenses.

The first man is fictionally named Frank Jennings. Mr. Jennings appears confident, trim, and clean shaven. Sartorially on message, he is wearing a pristine white shirt, a well-fitted jacket, and a tasteful tie. Seated behind a desk, he is looking unrepentant, despite his failure to act with integrity when he accessed customers' complaints based on his perception of their character without properly reviewing their circumstances.

From Mr. Jennings's expression of entitlement, I'm not surprised to learn by reading the case study that he refused to cooperate with the regulator during the course of the investigation. Indeed, so very confident looking is Mr. Jennings that he must have been genuinely perplexed when he was fined and banned.

The second of the two case studies illustrates another type of crime, this one having to do with bribery and corruption. The convicted man is identified only as Doughie; it has been decided that he doesn't deserve a last name.

Doughie is a stocky man wearing casual attire consisting of loosely fitted shirt and pants, both in black. The impression given is that this man probably has a single suit hanging in his closet in case he has to attend a funeral. Rather than sitting behind a desk, Doughie is standing with one hand in his pants' pocket as the other is gesticulating defensively. Looking at us with an expression of *I should have known better,* he recounts his tale of woe.

"I let my firm down, and they decided to let me go. Not that they got off so scot-free . . . I now have a criminal record . . . My wife stood by me at the start. Then she left. She took the house and the kids."

—

IN A TIME when actors are enlisted to instruct us with an online video on how not to cheat in life, Jordan Belfort has proven that life can go one step further by imitating acting and then by charging for it. Belfort, who was an actual trader, became the basis for the character played by Leonardo DiCaprio in the movie *The Wolf of Wall Street*. Having cheated countless people of millions of dollars, and after serving twenty-two months in prison, Belfort—are you ready—became a motivational speaker.

To explore Mr. Belfort's metamorphosis, and the staggering chutzpah that enabled it, I log on to his website. The home page features a dignified logo with his name in stately Garamond typeface, under which appears a tagline: "Corporate Training, Sales & Wealth Building Strategies." At the bottom of the page are links to "Private Bookings," "Products," and a "World Tour"; the last lists dates for his upcoming appearances in São Paulo, Bangkok, and Moscow.

The website also includes a videoed interview during which Mr. Belfort reveals that "anyone can bounce back from devastating setbacks, anyone can master the art of persuasion, and anyone can build massive wealth." If you are in doubt of any of this, Mr. Belfort gives his personal word: "It's all true. All real. All tested and proven to work." A sales pitch appears on the next screen page for a home study course, which teaches how to "ethically persuade anyone to take action."

Unprepared—and, frankly, unwilling—to spend a day with Jordan by attending one of his world tour seminars, I decide to subscribe to his newsletter. The first one gives me a sense of what is in store for me on a weekly basis.

Hi Eden,

A Chinese restaurant menu can offer well over 100 different dishes. At first glance that menu can look overwhelming with so many choices. . . . I want to look

at the choices we make and what we can do to remove
some stress.
    Click here to join me.
All the best,
Jordan

Finding a Chinese restaurant offering over a hundred dishes is unlikely even in China, but far more unsettling than the inaccuracy of Jordan's Chinese dish count is contemplating the probability of a universal truth—that money does not motivate the best in people. Christine Lagarde, the managing director of the International Monetary Fund, believes that a number of the world's financial systems were mired in scandal that violated "the most basic ethical norms" and that this will change only when stability and prudence are prized over greed.

I am hard put to be persuaded that there is much that prevails over greed, but every so often—in the least predictable way, and in the most unexpected place—there appears someone who decides to do the right thing.

7

PROS AND CONS OF DOING THE RIGHT THING

Integrity sells for so little, but it's all we have
left in this place. It is the very last inch of
us . . . but within that inch we are free.

—*Alan Moore,* V for Vendetta

When morality is pitted against profit, morality sustains itself
only as long as we are determined to do the right thing. We
might wish to do the right thing. We might aspire to a greater
good. We might admire excellence. But in our day-in and day-
out lives, we struggle with what is less than good or less than
excellent, while our apathy vies for supremacy. I intend to discuss this fallibility with Michael Woodford, the president and
CEO who blew the whistle on Olympus, the global company
he was running.

Established in 1919, Olympus forged its reputation as
a diversified, multinational corporation long before Mr.
Woodford assumed his post as its president in 2011. Japanese executives have been historically challenged when it
comes to implementing change within their businesses, and
it was not considered unusual when the board decided that
the task of revitalizing Olympus—with its forty-five thousand
employees—required a *gaijin,* a foreigner. After Mr. Woodford
worked his way up the ranks during the course of some thirty
previous years at Olympus, his promotion to president was

sponsored by the board's chairman, who, at the time, believed that the company was in need of a reset.

Shortly after Mr. Woodford assumed his post, an unnamed Olympus employee passed damaging information about the corporation to a Japanese freelance business writer who proceeded to identify three companies acquired by Olympus for $1 billion that had little or no value. The writer also discovered that the company had paid a disproportionately large financial advisory fee of $680 million for the services of an unknown consultant for an acquisition made some two years earlier. What the writer was unable to do was to sell the story to any one of the major Japanese media outlets, not because he could not substantiate the facts (he did), but because the Japanese media is self-censoring and no mainline domestic news organization would want to raise awkward questions about an iconic Nikkei-listed company like Olympus. The story eventually ran in *FACTA,* a maverick business publication, independent of the—some would claim incestuous—world of corporate Japan.

Despite its serious allegations of long-term malfeasance within one of Japan's largest and most important companies, the story was not picked up by the mainstream media in Japan, nor, it seems, did it cause concern at Olympus. In fact, Mr. Woodford was unaware of the article until a Japanese friend (who, at the time, was a board member of another one of Japan's largest companies) alerted him to it and then translated it for him (Mr. Woodford does not speak or read Japanese).

Mr. Woodford questioned a trusted executive on his senior management team about the information in the article and discovered that the chairman had instructed the executive—along with other members of Woodford's staff—not to discuss the article with anyone, Woodford included. Determined to pursue the issue on his own, Mr. Woodford wrote a series of six letters to his board colleagues seeking answers, in a forensic way, as to exactly what had taken place. He also commissioned the London practice of the accounting firm of Pricewaterhouse Coopers to investigate the charges. When its report helped evi-

dence a $1.7 billon fraud and confirmed that the company's
framework of governance had broken down, Mr. Woodford
made the audacious move of demanding the resignation of
the astounded chairman. In response, the board ratified the
chairman's resolution—read out loud and in front of Mr.
Woodford—that stripped Woodford of his title of president
and CEO; both titles were reassumed by the chairman. Mr.
Woodford told me that throughout the meeting not one of the
directors—some of whom he'd known for thirty years—made
eye contact with him.

THE FOLLOWING DAY, Mr. Woodford went public. His disclosures not only revealed the failures at Olympus; they shone
light on questionable Japanese corporate practices. They also
pointed a finger at Japan's press, which had compliantly looked
the other way. As for Mr. Woodford, he was vilified in Japan
when the company's share price lost over 80 percent of its value,
with $7 billion wiped off its market value.

I might make an observation that puts in perspective Mr.
Woodford's personality, and I should preface it by saying that
America is not a culture that rewards the self-effacing and that
Mr. Woodford has a way about him more American than British. He is not so much rude as determined, and I suspect that
same trait of purpose was responsible for his steadfast determination to do what he did.

On an unseasonably hot afternoon in June, Mr. Woodford
appears at my apartment meticulously dressed and unaffected
by the heat. He is in his mid-fifties, square-jawed, with razory
dark eyes, and black hair that has begun its retreat from his
forehead.

Thus far, those I've interviewed appear more willing to
speak freely when hospitality and food are offered. It is with
this in mind that I set out a pitcher of iced tea and a plate of
roasted pistachio nuts and pecorino cheese on the ottoman in

front of Mr. Woodford. He doesn't touch the food and, somewhat grim-faced, asks about the iced tea. I tell him I made it
with fresh mint, and as I am saying these words, I realize it
might be more a ladies' drink. We circle each other with small
talk until I volunteer that I've lived in China, where *mianzi*, or
"saving face," is an acknowledgment of dignity; that dignity in
the East is often more important than money; and that despite
the contentious differences that continue to exist between
Japan and China, I might have thought that they share this
cultural hallmark.

"In the case of Olympus, where was the Japanese sense of
honor and shame?" I ask.

"The shame was seen as upon me, not upon them. Most
Japanese business leaders would feel, even now, that I betrayed
the company, and that those involved were acting for the good
of the enterprise. White-collar crime is not perceived in the
way a violent crime would be; there are no victims as such."

By my count, in these circumstances, there were victims.
The Olympus board had been misstating the worth of the
company, and by doing so, it was undermining the value of
the stock. The secret it was keeping was at the expense of the
shareholders and the public.

"Not if the secret doesn't come out," replies Mr. Woodford
with a mirthless chuckle. "Fraud was constructed to hide the
losses from investing in very high-risk securities, the values of
which collapsed from the end of the bubble in Japan."

But that was over two decades before the disclosure. I put
it to him that there was nothing honorable about three of the
company's presidents passing a baton of misappropriated corporate funds, one to the other.

"That's a perspective you may take as a Westerner. The
general view is that what is expected in Japan is unconditional
loyalty to the hierarchy . . . to the company."

Mr. Woodford explains that the Japanese sense of honor
rested on the belief that virtue was enjoined by the higher calling of protecting the company. He points out that the com-

pany's corporate officers and directors understood exactly what was expected of them: it was to protect the chairman, to whom they were all loyal.

"Old generation, new generation, the values in Japan are held solidly," Mr. Woodford says.

"Not by the original whistle-blower, who contacted the freelance journalist," I remind him.

"He was the rare, honorable exception," says Mr. Woodford. "That man is still working at Olympus. Not even his wife knows he was the whistle-blower. She would have judged her husband the same way they judged me—as someone who betrayed the company."

I tell him that this strikes me as wholly absurd.

"Westerners can be ignorant of the mentality of Japan" is his somewhat dismissive reply.

"Well, okay, but weren't you just that kind of Westerner? After working for Olympus for some three decades and knowing what you knew of the Japanese culture, might you have chosen a more culturally conducive approach, one, perhaps, more subtle?"

His folded hands unfold to register impatience.

"There was nothing subtle in this case" is his defense. "How can you pay $1 billion for three companies without any turnover? Anyone can look at the facts of that. I was the company's president and an officer of the company, and to me what had happened was overwhelmingly wrong."

I wondered why, at the time, Mr. Woodford hadn't realized that, metaphorically speaking, the train had left the station three presidents ago. The Japanese sense of *right* was to stick to the train schedule; Mr. Woodford's version of *right* was to stop the train and announce that not only would the train be rerouted to an uncertain destination but that the captain—whom everyone knew and trusted—had been shoved off the train. True, Mr. Woodford's stance for the truth was brave. Still, one might have predicted that his chairman would react the way he did when confronted with Mr. Woodford's demand that he step down.

"What about the realities outside of the boardroom?" I ask him.

"Yes, well, there were two factors there. One was the degree of deference shown by Japanese media toward Japanese businesses. Had they probed and questioned, they would have been perceived as attacking corporate Japan. The second was the institutional investors, who withheld public criticism of the incumbent board and offered me no support as the deposed president fighting to bring out the truth. They seemed far more concerned that I was drawing attention to the issue than addressing what had been confirmed to be a fraud approaching $2 billion. And so it wasn't just the companies; it's the institutions around them."

MR. WOODFORD EXPLAINS that the Dodd-Frank Wall Street reform act bars retaliation against whistle-blowers. But my impression is that despite his multimillion-dollar out-of-court settlement Mr. Woodford, still aggrieved, is only a few objections away from becoming agitated all over again.

"At the end of dinner one night, the wife of one of my friends told me, 'You've subjected your wife and children to the consequences of your righteous ideas . . . and I think that's unforgivable.' I was thrown by what she said, but I respected her honesty, and in some sense I understand where it was coming from. When I meet other whistle-blowers, I tell them that even though that one decision has been a seismic event in their lives, it's a mistake to define yourself by it. Your business colleagues are unlikely to see it the way you have. And in the larger scheme of things, other people aren't that interested in what you've done and why. It might have been because of my own arrogance, but I misjudged those closest to me professionally, and, remember, this is thirty years working with these people. With some it had moved into close friendships. That taught me something."

After Mr. Woodford leaves my apartment, I contemplate the disillusioned "something" in his parting sentence. Is it that whistle-blowers are almost never envied? Is it that doing the right thing puts the established order at risk? Perhaps it's the realization that what binds us together is not so much virtue as the fear of losing our security.

8

THE LAW: TOOLS OF CONTROL, OR INSTRUMENTS OF ENLIGHTENMENT?

Justice?—You get justice in the next world,
in this world you have the law.

—*William Gaddis*, A Frolic of His Own

Unlike Michael Woodford, I've yet to be called on to speak out publicly against a wrong. I have, however, faced down a number of institutional and legal absurdities. One in particular presented itself when I was a book publisher in New York.

"The State of New York wants to speak to you," said my assistant, who, rather than using the intercom on her desk phone, came into my office to make the stunning announcement.

"I don't understand" was, not surprisingly, my reaction.

"I'm not kidding," she insisted. "That's what the man said. He's holding on line 2."

THE MAN ON line 2 was from the prosecuting attorney's office and proceeded to cite chapter and verse of the Son of Sam law, passed by the State of New York to prevent criminals from profiting from their crimes by writing about them.

"We—that is the State of New York—are in the lawful

position to appropriate and distribute the royalty revenue from an autobiography you're publishing entitled *The Mayflower Madam*."

"Just out of curiosity, to whom would you distribute the money?" I asked.

"To the victims of the crimes committed by your author."

This struck me as humorous, and I was warned that it was no laughing matter.

It wasn't that I disagreed with the principle behind the law, but given the circumstances it was a challenge this time to identify the intent of the law. The author in question was Sydney Biddle Barrows, dubbed "the *Mayflower* Madam" thanks to her social pedigree; her ancestors landed on Plymouth Rock with the first English settlers. Ms. Barrows was a madam whose clients, unnamed in her best-selling memoir, had been happy to pay for the company of the young women in her service, many of whom were medical, business, and, ironically, law students looking to earn money while studying. Ms. Barrows dressed her charges in discreet attire purchased at Bergdorf Goodman, possibly the most elegant clothes store in Manhattan, and instructed them to read *Forbes* and the *Wall Street Journal* so that they were able to hold their own outside the boudoir. I was not denying that the law against prostitution had been broken, but who, exactly, were the victims when the clients were paying a great deal of money—sometimes thousands of dollars—for a private arrangement? Might it have been that the State of New York was coming after what it had convinced itself was its fair share?

The legal and moral question of what to do—or not to do—about prostitution is as old as the trade, with laws moving in both directions and influenced not so much by a dereliction of moral standards as by economics. When, for example, large numbers of men and women abandoned the French countryside between 1850 and 1870, trade and industry formed a new class of wealth in Paris, the city almost doubled in population, and traditional social codes were replaced with moral tolerance and prostitution became legal, so much so that it utilized its own currency in the form of tokens. The point is that morality is often lost on ground level, which is why I am beginning to suspect the theory of sin was utilized as a tool for controlling human behavior. Under God's all-seeing eye, any questionable occurrence or inclination—even those not breaking the law— had the potential of becoming a sin. But while religion teaches to love thy neighbor, and not to covet thy neighbor's wife, it is the law and the law alone we turn to when that neighbor takes a free ride on our financial benevolence or encroaches on our property.

The Mesopotamian Code of Hammurabi, preserved on stone columns and dating back to the mid-eighteenth century B.C., lists 282 laws, nearly half of which address matters of contract such as wages and property. A third of the code consists of provisions concerning marriage, inheritance, divorce, and paternity. With issues of inheritance, it wasn't until the eleventh century that the law stood on its own as a stabilizing force: largely the result of continuous warfare over land. Within a system of landownership, property cascaded down as inheritance to the firstborn son, and laws prevented illegitimate heirs from intruding on the family unit on which property was centered.

Many hundreds of years later, testing the laws of inheritance and property in a way to remember were the 1920s divorce proceedings in the U.K. of *Russell v. Russell*—a case that hinged on the sexual relationship (or, more accurately, the lack of sexual relationship) between a married couple. For his part, John Russell insisted that he had no interaction of an intimate nature with his wife, Christabel, and that the baby she gave birth to was illegitimate. Christabel explained that at the time of conception she and her husband were guests in a house that was limited to a single bathroom between them. She recounted how she had taken a bath in the same tub as her husband not long after he did. She also used the sponge he had.

By now, you might be asking yourself any number of questions, the least having to do with a bathtub or a sponge. In the eyes of the law, both were crucial to the case.

The theory canvassed in the court and enjoyed by the press was that John had pleasured himself while taking his bath, which explained how, according to Christabel's attorney, she became pregnant while soaking in her husband's recently vacated tub and sponging, as she did, her nether regions.

I have absolute faith in the transformative properties of a long soak in the bath, but the outcome of this one was a triumph of imagination in the service of property. Hilariously funny as it might be now, then the gynecological impossibility of Christabel Russell's pregnancy was given not only legal credence but also a name: the paternity of the "Sponge Baby" was upheld.

For the majority not grappling with the upmarket issues of inheritance, the promise of moral justice presented itself in the late eighteenth century with utilitarianism and its proposition that being good isn't a question for an individual but a measurement of the greatest happiness of the greatest number of people. The founder of utilitarianism, Jeremy Bentham, was a leading theorist in the philosophy of law who advocated separation of church and state, freedom of expression, equal rights for women and their right to divorce, the decriminalizing of homosexual acts, and the abolition of slavery and of the death penalty.

The principle of utilitarianism is not reflected in the Universal Declaration of Human Rights and America's Bill of Rights. Instead, both enlist the rights-based ethics system, ensuring that the rights of a single person have greater importance than the happiness of the many. This system presents ethical challenges of its own. It is why Abu Qatada al-Filistini, allegedly affiliated with al-Qaeda and detained in the U.K. under anti-terrorism laws, was released from custody when the U.K. had no specific reason to prosecute him for a crime, and it explains how the European Court of Human Rights barred the U.K.

from deporting Abu Qatada to Jordan, a country determined to put him on trial. Eventually, Abu Qatada was extradited, but only after the U.K. and Jordanian governments ratified a treaty satisfying the U.K.'s Human Rights Act (guaranteeing fundamental rights and freedoms entitled in the U.K.) that no torture would be used in Jordan to gain evidence against him in his forthcoming trial. All of this caused a great many U.K. citizens to reconsider the validity of an ethical system based on an individual's rights.

According to Edie Weiner this is fast becoming the case in America as well.

Ms. Weiner is acknowledged in the United States as one of the most influential practitioners of social, technological, and political trend spotting. She believes that even America—a nation whose forebearers escaped the scourge of economic, political, and religious oppression that existed in other countries—is struggling with its rights-based system. I return to New York with the intention of meeting Ms. Weiner.

Landing from London in the early afternoon New York time the day prior to our meeting—and determined not to succumb to the time difference—I take a long walk in order to stay awake. Manhattan is a vertical place, less than ten miles long and three miles wide, where the haves and have-nots live cheek by jowl. Not far from where I am staying downtown, a group of homeless men are milling around what I can see is a lineup of black chauffeured cars out of which occasionally step thin, well-dressed white women; it occurs to me that this must be the afternoon pickup at a private school. Made curious by the school, when I return from my walk, I phone someone I know who might be familiar with it. She informs me that the school's fees hover at the $45,000-a-year mark but that its moral mission statement promises to instill in the students humility about their personal advantages. I am very much hoping that tomorrow Edie Weiner might help me understand how this is believed possible.

When I arrive at Ms. Weiner's midtown office, she instructs

me to sit on one side of the couch with her on the other so we're
not seated across from each other with her behind a desk. With
a tristate accent that drops vowels and urban self-possession,
Ms. Weiner first wants to make sure I understand what I've
managed to conclude on my own: that morality differs from
ethics, but that neither is the same thing as justice.

"And there's no guarantee justice and the law are the same,"
she warns.

"Still, most of us think of the law as a moral instrument,"
say I.

"Okay," she says with a glint in her eye. "If that's where you
want to go, I'll follow you down that rabbit hole. Let's use the
example of business and contract law."

Despite being somewhat taken aback by her forceful
approach, I feel confident that I'll be able to keep pace with the
point Ms. Weiner is about to convey—this because I've negotiated contracts, often in challenging circumstances.

"I'm ready," I tell her.

"In Western law, the contract is a dead instrument" is
how she begins. "Once it's signed, that's it: if one party breaks
it, they're liable for the damages. But with more and more
women in law, there's been a shift of sorts," says Ms. Weiner.
When women are involved in the legal process, they tend to be
interested in justice; when men are involved, they tend to
be interested in enforcing the law."

Ms. Weiner's statement on women entering the legal profession is not inaccurate: according to Ruth Bader Ginsburg,
who has served as an associate justice of the Supreme Court of
the United States since 1993, about half the nation's law students and more than one-third of the federal judges are women.
Still, her comment about men and women and the process of
law makes me sit up a bit, and I am eyeing her closely as she
continues.

"Sticking with the example of a contract, it's not unusual
for a woman judge to say, basically, 'Wait a minute—let's
think about this. Why was the contract broken? Maybe it

was a bad contract to begin with, or maybe the circumstances have changed and you *should* have broken the contract.' This changes things. As soon as a judge wants to know the story, the contract is no longer dead; it becomes a living instrument. Businesses that thought they had something sealed and done find themselves liable in the court of law. And this is how it becomes no longer about the law but about justice."

I nod that I've followed her point.

"Now we go deeper down the rabbit hole," she says. "In business, the corporation is the 'legal envelope' into which the business is tucked. What the corporation does is to shield its executives from personal liability, which is why the corporation, as a legal entity, is not necessarily perceived as justice. And because there is often a blur between law and morality or ethics, there are things people think they can get away with until the law tells them, specifically, 'You can't do that.'"

I ask Ms. Weiner if she thinks human nature—greed, in particular—instigates our attempts to outwit the law.

"It's many people's human nature to do precisely that, and many people's not to," she says. "Selfishness cannot be kept in check without altruism, and humankind can't progress without the two: selfishness and altruism. It's only when the two are in balance that we get ahead."

"And morality?"

"Morality is what you're answerable to within yourself, whatever that higher order is . . . something exercised by an individual that says to him or her, 'Even though this is not against the law, I shouldn't do this.'"

"What about ethics?"

"Ethics exist in order to bind together people in a given society by providing behavioral consistency and solidarity. Ethics have penalties attached if you don't abide by them. Ethics are situational. They're opportunistic. They're politically based and are dictated by people with power in a particular arena. It could be business. It could be the law. It could be the military."

I tell Ms. Weiner that from what I've seen in my travels, ethics are almost entirely relative to place. China performs executions on a regular basis; America does so now and again, depending on state-by-state legal variants. Most countries in Europe never do. The Middle East is a veritable execution bazaar. Are Europeans the most moral? I want to know, but instead ask Ms. Weiner if she thinks there's validity in moral absolutes.

"People have a societal take on moral absolutes," she tells me. "I think that's why people in America who can afford it are moving into communities that are like-minded. Unfortunately, those like-minded communities are breeding future generations of people who believe as they do, as opposed to a broader-thinking society of mixed races and religions. It's what's pulling us apart."

An idealist who grew up in the 1970s, at one time Ms. Weiner embraced the belief that separate cultures in a shared, diverse society should merit equal respect and an equal say. Now she wonders whether, in its rush to accommodate multiculturalism, America's ideology has led to its institutional and political failure.

To many, this might be construed as an un-American way of thinking; after all, the pursuit of happiness is a cornerstone of America's Declaration of Independence. But while it's true that no other country but America has evolved so many different ways for citizens to remain individuals, it's also true that its conflicting values have created a polarized climate. I ask Ms. Weiner how, in a nation's racial and cultural mishmash, she proposes we reframe moral issues.

"You leave the word 'morality' out, and you bring in the word 'culture,'" she tells me.

"Let's talk about culture," I suggest. "When cultures had their own clearly defined national borders, the definition of what was moral and what was ethical made sense within those borders. Globalization has shrunk physical distance, but the same cannot be said about cultural chasms. Ours is an era of churn, with more displaced people than ever before, many fleeing to countries with very different moralities. Do we force cultural and moral integration in order for everyone to become more like *us*?"

Ms. Weiner lingers in frowning concentration, and when she answers, it is in a roundabout way, but one that is also clear.

"I grew up in foster homes among people with the same religion, in the same community, in the same era. Still, each time I changed families, I was instructed to adhere to a different *absolute* way to do things, to act, to think. What we come to believe is absolute is nothing more than the reality in our minds."

Ms. Weiner remarks that America is a nation that takes from every culture in the world and builds on an incredibly wide range of moralities.

"We have more people from other countries than some of the host countries they come from. America has been absorbing this type of universality since the time it was born," she tells me, before suggesting that America might have an advantage over other countries when it comes to the thorny issues today of assimilating an unrelenting flow of immigrants and refugees.

"If you take a look at the Netherlands, for example—always praised for being so liberal and open—what do you think is happening there, with almost one million Muslims?"

I'm not sure what is actually happening in the Netherlands, but from Ms. Weiner's condemnatory tone, I assume it involves backpedaling.

She tells me that, when the number of Muslims shifted upward there, a white supremacy movement emerged. "In the Netherlands," she repeats, shaking her head. "Of all places."

It's not only the Netherlands, what had been Denmark's equally progressive self-image is beginning to buckle. Some 36,000 predominately Muslim asylum seekers have poured into that small country, and its native population is beginning to resent newcomers putting a strain on its social-welfare system while failing to adapt to its customs.

Ms. Weiner and I sit in momentary silence, and then a wan smile creeps across her face.

Hers is a world-weary sense of humor when she tells me that the solution to those who seem to be open-minded is to allow a few into their club; it's never to join the other club.

"As long as the numbers don't swing to the other side, everyone can feel morally wonderful."

She points out that Muslims are procreating at a rate of ten to one in the developed world, making demographic change in other countries inevitable because, at the same time, the native born are aging. We fall into agreement that what will eventually counter the current generation's insular instincts are their children. Young people will continue to flock to vibrant cities for employment, and they will have a very different take from their parents on issues that come with a mixed demographic.

"But what happens until then? What about now?" I ask.

Ms. Weiner tells me that people should not be forced to relinquish their cultural identity when they immigrate but that a more effective approach to cultural integration is required than currently exists. She tells me that there are two important things to understand about a culture: its rewards and its punishments. America—a nation whose founding principles recognized the individual—has not forsaken the individual, but it has become less concerned with that individual's background, his or her beliefs, and what he or she learned at home or in church.

"In effect, our country's policies and laws are beginning to say that if you want to belong, these are the rules. We don't care about your Confederate flag, your religious beliefs, your sexual beliefs—these are the rules of this cultural society. Get used to it."

She stares intensely at the floor and then looks up with an expression that tugs at sadness.

"That won't rid us of prejudice," she tells me. "People will always need to create *others*."

Leaving Ms. Weiner's office during Manhattan's rush hour, I join a dense herd of humanity trying to get home. As I head toward the bus stop down the block, a shrill sound of angry horns is directed at a man holding up traffic by double-parking his truck. A cabdriver, stuck directly behind the truck, has gotten out of his cab, presumably to take his complaint directly to the source of the problem. The two men begin to shout at each other: not an unusual method of expression on New York City streets. As an on-and-off New Yorker, I, too, have, on occasion, handled my own skirmishes there with a variety of unattractive words, but what the truck driver yells at the dark-skinned cabdriver shocks me to the core.

"Get out of my country!" is what I hear for the first time in a city where virtually everyone has come from some other place.

Wedged in a crowded express bus inching downtown, I mull over how the truck driver might have convinced himself that America belongs to only his kind, whatever he perceives his kind to be. I wonder if he is aware that whites have dropped below half of all Americans under the age of five. He might even know—but is too angry or afraid to admit—that, despite the promises made to him by politicians, nothing can prevent the modern world's unrelenting mass mobility, and that it is the combination of *others* that will imagine our future.

9

THE POLITICAL FUNCTION OF ETHICS

Politics have no relation to morals.

—*Niccolò Machiavelli*

There have been mass shootings in the United States during the months I've lived in London. Left in their bloody wake is the nonnegotiable American right to purchase semiautomatic rifles whose sole purpose is to kill as many people in the shortest time possible. Gun violence in America is the result of choices uniquely American—choices that have made my own country almost unrecognizable to me. This was certainly the case with my trip to New York: it coincided with the presidential run-up.

The U.S. electoral process is unlike that in the U.K., which regulates campaign spending and holds candidates and their parties to a short period of debate and canvassing: not a perfect system, but one that manages to reduce the number of political footholds for special interest groups. Full disclosure covers even the royal family, whose interaction with civic society is noted on a daily basis in the *Times* in what is referred to as the Court Circular. One can learn, for instance, that the Duke of Gloucester, who is royal patron of the Peace and Prosperity Trust, will be attending the Building Bridges Through Culture concert to celebrate the fifteenth anniversary of the Arab International Women's Forum at Kensington Palace State Apartments. Laugh if you wish, but lacking the kind of compliance and transparency employed in the British electoral process, America's political parties in an election year align their strategic decisions more with math than morality. And while it is true that politicians—regardless of nationality—have proven willing to drag decency through the muck, it seems to me that there's more restraint in expressing that intention in the U.K. Offering a lesson on the political effectiveness of English understatement was the former Labour leadership contender, David Miliband. When asked what he thought about that party's representative, Jeremy Corbyn, personally, Miliband conveyed his sentiments in an exhilaratingly rude way, without being uncouth.

"Apparently, he is nice to his cats" was all that needed to be said on the matter.

I HAVE REENTERED America at a time when presidential candidate/real estate mogul/reality television celebrity Donald Trump appears to have orchestrated a hostile takeover of the Republican Party. Granted, I've arrived from a country where the most aggressively personal thing I've heard a public figure say about someone else in the public eye was Sir Nicholas Soames calling Julian Assange a "scoundrel liar coward bail fugitive and common criminal," but nothing could have prepared me for Mr. Trump. He is mesmerizingly reprehensible. Just when I think that his personal attacks couldn't possibly be more lewd, or his view of his fellow human more lacking in humanity, he is somehow able to find new and amazing ways to do both, often at the same time. Adding a surreal touch to his verbal incontinence are proposed policies beyond the imaginings of a coked-up Hollywood screenwriter. That Trump spouts pants-on-fire lies, backed by totally wrong information, doesn't seem to matter. And here, to be fair, I must point out that, in this regard, the United States and the U.K. are not that dissimilar: the two countries are now equally comfortable with a post-factual democracy. After Britain's prime minister reck-lessly called for a referendum to separate from the European Union, many of that nation's otherwise pragmatic people—feeling marginalized by globalization—are willing to ignore the data on the economic advantages of a free movement of labor.

LIKE AMERICA, THE U.K. is beginning to pull up its draw-bridges. And as is the case among more and more Americans, there's a growing aversion to experts among the British. When it was pointed out that almost all of the research indicated that immigration aids—rather than undermines—economic growth, a leader in that campaign stated that he thought peo-ple have had enough of experts.

Donald Trump is one of those people. Though not a U.K. citizen, he owns a golf course in Scotland, which, according to him, "is like running a country." The number of times Mr. Trump's businesses have filed for bankruptcy is four, but we can rest assured of his profitable ownership of the Miss Amer-ica contest. Admitting to reading almost nothing, he explains the forces that will influence him when, as the next American president, he commands the U.S. Armed Forces and controls their nuclear codes.

"I'm speaking with myself, number one, because I have a good brain and I've said a lot of things."

DESPITE—OR POSSIBLY BECAUSE of—Trump's consistently deranged discourse and offensive, needlessly cruel rhetoric, money is to be made, and the media is willing to be exploited. Voracious, twenty-four-hour news channels are on a feedback loop of sound bites, while polls provide filler material—polls having to do not with the issues but with the feelings of the electorate. According to one, Hillary Clinton—whose entitlement has nurtured the scandals in which she is now mired—is considered an untrustworthy person, but those same people polled think that her untrustworthiness won't affect her ability to lead. If that doesn't make one wonder about the bankruptcy of morality in politics, Mr. Trump's views do: they are marinated in misogyny, racism, and belittlement of the disabled. That he is in a position to state untruths as if unimpeachable facts to foster resentment among a sizable number of the public has brokered no favors to China's pro-democracy reformers. Just the opposite: it has lent credence to the one-party system's belief that giving people the right to vote would not be a wise decision.

With words that taunt what was once considered unspeakable and tactics that jump the rails, Trump insists he is on the side of those unemployed or struggling from paycheck to paycheck whose plights have been ignored by the status quo. The rallying cry of renewed domestic glory, "Make America Great Again," circulates on social media where increasingly Americans consume their information. Navigating around traditional media and their fact-checking, his outreach on Twitter and Facebook is saturated with promises to those who have been economically marginalized by globalization and are made anxious by America's shift in demographics.

Recalling something that H. L. Mencken's wrote: "As democracy is perfected, the office represents, more and more closely, the inner soul of the people," and convinced that a xenophobic reality program celebrity vying to become U.S. President cannot possibly reflect the soul of my country or hold the answer to its shortcomings, I return to the U.K. for a hastily scheduled meeting and a different example of the democratic process.

KNOWN AS AGWAMBO (the Mysterious One), the Right Honorable Raila Odinga is a controversial politician in his own country of Kenya and an enigma even to his supporters. From what I've read, he appears to be a man who believes that the ideal of democracy is a universal concept, and he has paid for that belief from a Kenyan jail.

I have managed to make contact with Mr. Odinga's inner circle in advance of his trip to London, where he is scheduled to speak at Chatham House, the Royal Institute of International Affairs. He has agreed to lunch with me after his speech. His daughter, who is in her mid-twenties, will be joining us.

WE ARE SEATED on the terrace of a private club, chosen for no other reason than its two-block proximity to Chatham House. As soon as the waiter has completed our orders, I ask my guests for a short tutorial on Kenya's history.

As early as the first century, port town communities in what would become Kenya formed the region's city-states, which were eventually part of an expansive trade network and served as facilitators to Arab, Persian, Indian, Chinese, and Indonesian merchants. The colonial history of Kenya began in 1885 with the establishment of a German protectorate. On its heels was the arrival of the Imperial British East Africa Company.

It is believed that the origin of the name Kenya is linked to one of three words in three native languages—*Kirinyago, Kirenyaa,* and *Kiinyaa*—all sharing the same meaning: God's Resting Place. The British claimed it as their own, and here I am reminded of how Eddie Izzard, the British performer, explains the English's method of building their empire "by stealing countries with the stunning use of flags." By the 1930s, the country's central highlands had been settled by British and European farmers, one of whom depicted her experience pseudonymously as Isak Dinesen in an autobiographical book, *Out of Africa.*

Seven years of the decade that was the 1950s kept Kenya in a state of emergency from the Mau Mau rebellion against

British rule. The U.K. ceded sovereignty in 1963; a year later, Kenya became a republic. A year after that, Jomo Kenyatta was named the first president of independent Kenya.

As the country's founding father, Kenyatta failed to form a homogeneous state with his one-party rule. He bequeathed Kenya its de facto status of a confederation of competing tribal interests that hindered a political consensus. By ruling with and through a consortium largely of his relatives and the offspring of former colonial chiefs, President Kenyatta was responsible for the formation of the nation's wealthiest and most influential class.

"KENYA HAS HAD a rocky road to democracy," Mr. Odinga tells me.

This is an understatement, given both Kenya's political history and Mr. Odinga's background, which are in certain parts one and the same.

Mr. Odinga's father was a prominent figure in Kenya's struggle for independence from the British and the country's first vice president under President Kenyatta in its one-party state. He fell out with President Kenyatta when he formed an opposition party.

Truth be told, I have difficulty keeping straight who in Kenya has jailed whom and for what reason, particularly in the case of Raila Odinga. With evidence pointing to his collaboration with plotters of a failed coup attempt against Kenya's second president in 1982 (and in which thousands of rebel soldiers were killed), Mr. Odinga was placed under house arrest and then charged with treason and detained in prison without a trial. After six years of incarceration, he was released and rearrested seven months later—the result, he has told me, of pressing for human rights and a multiparty democracy in Kenya (at the time, still a one-party state). He was released in 1989, only to be incarcerated yet again a year later.

—

MR. ODINGA INTERRUPTS the narrative by asking the waiter if he might remove his coat. Granted permission to be more comfortable in the outdoor humidity, he resumes the story: when he was released nearly a year after being jailed a third time, he fled the country to Norway at the prompting of what I am led to believe was an unsuccessful attempt to assassinate him.

In 1992, Mr. Odinga returned to Kenya to push for a multiparty democracy and subsequently stood against the government-backed constitutional committee's draft of a constitution, which was perceived to consolidate powers of the presidency and weaken regional governments. Despite various death threats against Mr. Odinga, he accused the government of withholding identity cards from voters supportive of the opposition and launched his own presidential campaign.

Having lost the presidential election by fewer than 250,000 votes and convinced that he was robbed of victory, Mr. Odinga called for his supporters to protest in street demonstrations that turned violent and brought the country to the brink of collapse with more than 1,000 people killed and 660,000 displaced in ethnic clashes. Civil unrest ended when the former UN secretary-general Kofi Annan brokered a power-sharing post of prime minister for Mr. Odinga.

It was Kofi Annan whom Mr. Odinga quoted during his talk at Chatham House, the subject of which was the challenges of ensuring moral, political, and economic accountability given Kenya's relatively short experience of democracy.

"Democracy is not just about one day every four or five years when elections are held, but a system of government that respects the separation of powers, fundamental freedoms like the freedom of thought, religion, expression, association and assembly, and the rule of law. Any regime that rides roughshod on these principles loses its democratic legitimacy, regardless of whether it initially won an election" is Kofi Annan's warning repeated to me by Mr. Odinga.

Our main course arrives, along with an official at the club who informs Mr. Odinga that according to the club's rules he must put his jacket back on. I begin to object, but Mr. Odinga graciously does what is asked while telling me that despite the government's agreement to reform the Independent Electoral and Boundaries Commission, he believes there is still no real respect for a moral rule of law.

My question is, why is there so much entrenched corruption, not only in Kenya, but in Africa in general? I adjust the words to something more palatable.

"Do you really think politicians and government officials whose moral scorecard is precarious at best can be morally reasoned with?"

"As long as there are no consequences, they will not care," he tells me.

Mr. Odinga explains that initially a single purpose galvanized Kenya's culturally and tribally disparate nation.

"The political focus among Kenyans was to replace British rule. Once the republic was established, Kenya's political elites were granted power, and they allowed civil servants to profit from participation in the private sector. It took a toll, especially on bidding for building and construction. My point is that this mentality has been ingrained and what is needed now is a strong oversight authority. It will come only with institutions."

Mr. Odinga tells me that he wants the electoral commission in Kenya to step down and a new voters' register to be in place before the next general election. This is his preamble to what he insists is the obligation of the United States, the U.K., and the EU to play their part and back Kenya's efforts for a moral democracy. He says that elections in Kenya are being viewed with an extremely narrow focus on how peaceful the elections are and not on how free and fair they should be.

"The performance of incumbents is being judged by how

the West can use them to fight terrorism, regardless of the human rights abuses that accompany the fight."

I suggest that given the current political environment, especially in the United States, it is unlikely Kenya will receive the support he believes is a moral obligation.

"Perhaps the realistic and practical approach would be if Kenya were to take responsibility for itself and elect politicians more likely to think long term."

As soon as the words pass from my lips, I realize how hypocritical is the idea they express. The fact is, I can't locate the political function of ethics in my own country, where policies—especially foreign policies—are about the short term and rarely consider what might be possible.

Africa has had three female heads of state, and I ask Mr. Odinga's daughter if she believes women are more prone to think long term because they are likely mothers concerned with the world and a future in which their children will live.

"That's not an unreasonable premise," she tells me.

She also tells me that she will be working on behalf of her father's campaign.

"What campaign is that?" I ask, turning the question to Mr. Odinga.

"I am running in Kenya's upcoming presidential race," he answers, sounding not at all enigmatic. I ask about the presidential incumbent against whom he is running. It is Uhuru Kenyatta, the son of Kenya's first president, whose vice president broke with him. That man was Mr. Odinga's father, which makes the run for president a multi-generational enterprise.

BY THE END of our lunch, I'm not sure what Mr. Odinga's moral script is. I have, however, decided that, writ large, politics usher in vanity, folly, bravery, and ambition while morality is left to find its own way.

PART THREE

Sex as Moral Provocateur

10

MONOGAMY (NOT SO MUCH ANYMORE)

Is you is or is you ain't my baby?

—*from a 1944 Louis Jordan song*

Buried deep underground, spanning the border between Switzerland and France, is the largest scientific experiment ever constructed: the Large Hadron Collider. It is the work of ten thousand scientists—men and women—from across the globe, united in their quest to uncover the fundamental building blocks of our universe. A majority of these ten thousand people are—or have been—married. That means that in a single, life-changing act they have forfeited anything and everything that has to do with science, including the clearheaded knowledge that marriage is entirely dependent on the unrealistic premise that one person can hold the other person to the lifetime promise. Science, in its pure state, has no moral dimension.

Not so with marriage.

EVEN THOUGH MARRIAGE in the West has declined in every age cohort, the idea of marriage continues to hold sway. Societal attitudes of marital infidelity vary, however, and though most moral systems include a warning against adultery, prohibitions have proven inconsistent. Until outlawed in the eleventh century, polygamy was commonly practiced among Jews. Even Jesus, a profoundly important and lasting moral agent, took a "he who has not sinned can cast the first stone" stance when it came to the subject, and King Solomon, known to be the wisest of men, admitted without a second thought that he "loved strange women." Here, I think, we must assume that he yielded to the enchantments of sexual variety and meant "strange" as in diversity, rather than in temperament, for, purportedly, he had seven hundred wives and three hundred concubines—a testimony not only to his stamina but to an obvious talent for time management.

Solomon's sexual escapades are justified on the Mormon .org website, which states that "at various times, the Lord has commanded His people to practice plural marriage." Mentioned on the site are other lucky men given the same moral dispensation: Abraham, Isaac, Jacob, Moses, and David.

FOR CENTURIES, WESTERN expectations of marriage have been based on the impression that one person can meet all of the other's needs and wants. That has proven to be a losing proposition, with a significant number of men and women in America coming to the conclusion that the marriage bed is not where passion can be found. Demonstrating the serious disparity between marital infidelity and the societal attitudes toward it, research indicates that over the past two decades 21 percent of men and 10 to 15 percent of women have cheated on their partners, with that same study reporting that 91 percent of Americans believe infidelity is immoral.

Whether in America or in foreign countries, I have found it best to avoid making judgments on all matters pertaining to the subject of sex. Living in Brussels at one point, I knew to keep my thoughts to myself during a conversation with the pregnant woman seated next to me at a dinner. She was due to have her baby the following month.

"Will your husband attend the birth?" I asked. "That seems to be the case more and more in the States."

"He wasn't anywhere near during the conception. Why would I want him there for the birth?" was her straight-faced response, leaving no doubt that it was a lover with whom she became pregnant.

THE MALE PERSPECTIVE can be conveyed in equally blunt terms.

"I find it genuinely unreasonable that men should be confined to one woman," grumbled London's former (and married) mayor Boris Johnson when the media reported his personal affairs.

While some might file adultery under a mild form of mendacity, the French don't bother with filing it at all. Most Frenchwomen think it naive to divorce a husband for his infidelity. Nor would a Frenchwoman, having an affair with a married man and given the option to marry him, likely forget that when a man marries his mistress, it creates a vacancy for another mistress.

Though I enjoyed the confidence of mutual fidelity during my fifteen-year marriage, I don't believe infidelity should be designated an immoral act. Yes, it can cause torment. Yes, it almost always leaves in its wake crippling distrust. Yes, it is an unforgettably selfish abdication of responsibility for the person who loves you. And, yes, I agree with the French legal system, which has, from time to time, considered murder a crime of passion between spouses and lovers when provoked by infidelity. I agree because, with matters of the heart, I might very well have killed my husband upon discovering a betrayal. And, yes, that would have made for bad behavior on my part and poor judgment on his.

—

THERE ARE CULTURAL divides between what is considered moral in matters of marriage and what is thought to be poor judgment. In America, extramarital affairs often prevent politicians from high offices, and the country's presidents face harsh judgment from voters when there is the slightest hint of sexual impropriety. But in France, there seems to be a shield of moral invisibility that surrounds politicians when it comes to what would be scandalous behavior elsewhere, and French presidents have long been known for their extramarital affairs at no political cost. Indeed, it is expected.

Jacques Chirac's amorous propensities earned him a colorful reputation.

Valéry Giscard d'Estaing once crashed his car into a truck at dawn on a visit to a lover. François Mitterrand's funeral revealed his daughter by a mistress of thirty-four years. François Hollande shared the Élysée Palace with a woman to whom he was not married but who nonetheless acted as First Lady until the president was caught in a clandestine affair with a French actress. "He who has betrayed will betray" was the operatic declaration from the First Lady he threw over. True, but apparently beside the point. The point, it seemed, was that the president's comings and goings were on a scooter. That undignified fact was what tested France's tolerance toward its president, not issues having to do with what others might insist are moral shortcomings.

ACROSS THE ATLANTIC is a semi-French-speaking country, Canada, where Noel Biderman launched Ashley Madison, an international dating web service for married people wishing to be unfaithful. The website, whose tagline was "Life is short. Have an affair," has branded itself as a modern facilitator of infidelity.

Marketing itself as the face of acceptable infidelity, the Toronto-based company has taken an entire floor in a high-rise office building whose sleek, impersonal lobby offers no comfortable place to sit. Greeting me is the marketing director, one of few men on a staff of women of various ages under thirty.

In an attempt to up the cool factor, each of several conference rooms in the office features a brass plate engraved with the name of a famously unfaithful man; I am ushered into the Bill Clinton Room. Noel Biderman enters and approaches me as though walking toward an electric fence. Fair enough. I'd made the trip to Toronto with the express purpose of discussing the subject of morality, and he was, after all, the founder of a company with a moral taint.

Closing in on middle age, balding and with ambiguously presented facial hair, of average height and weight, Mr. Biderman is wearing a crisply checkered shirt, a bland gray blazer, generic white chinos, and brown suede loafers. His licorice-colored eyes do not look on me warmly. With minimally changing facial expression, he shares the details of his daily routine, which includes a can of Red Bull in the afternoon. That having been disclosed, I cannot say whether he is, by nature, a high-strung fellow, or it happens that our conversation is occurring at the caffeine-fueled apex of his day. Either way, the mechanical rat-a-tat-tat velocity of what he has to say reminds me of a ticker-tape machine. Given the line of business that he is in, I assume that he assumes that I will judge him morally lacking. His defense mechanism is to preemptively catalog my thoughts before I have the chance to express them. After he interrupts me for the third time, I try putting him at ease by concentrating our conversation on the neutral topic of starting a business.

Investors in the site's holding company (then calling itself Avid Life Media; now rebranded as ruby Corp.), are wealthy North Americans who prefer to remain anonymous. Sales have increased fourfold in the past five years, registering a profit margin between 20 and 25 percent, with revenue driven by a pay-as-you-play financial model. This means that there is no monthly subscription cost; instead, men pay for credits, which they then use for online introductions to women.

The most reasonably priced option for men logging on to the site is to purchase 100 credits for $55. This provides an equivalent of five hours of instant messaging time or twenty e-mails to others on the site. For those prepared to splurge, the premium program runs $360, offering six months of unlimited e-mailing and 750 credits, which equals about thirty-seven hours of instant messaging time. Clients can transfer credit to other clients, much like gifting frequent-flier miles.

The sentiment behind this ploy escapes me, and while it is true that I am not enamored of his self-satisfied personality, I'd be a fool to argue with Mr. Biderman's bottom-line results. According to what he is telling me, his company turned cash flow positive six months after the site was launched; its current fiscal year is estimated to close with a $150 million profit and it was valuing itself at $1 billion.

At one point in my career, I, too, launched a company, though a far less profitable one than Ashley Madison, and what I've read about him gives me no reason to doubt that Mr. Biderman—a former sports attorney—is a shrewd entrepreneur. He effectively monetized the site's thirty-seven million clients in some fifty-three countries (though the site is banned in South Korea and Singapore). That means that each day more than twenty-five thousand men and women were logging on to Ashley Madison with the self-published intention to be unfaithful. Monday morning, presumably when people return to work after a disappointing weekend, is its busiest time.

There's no mystery to having an illicit affair; adultery is one of the more banal human impulses. Neither of these two facts prevents Ashley Madison's site from including a "tips" section, offering advice for successful encounters.

Ashley Madison's home page features a full-frame photograph of a woman holding her finger to her lips, as if promising that the site will keep affairs hushed up. But in an era of hacking and leaked e-mails, would-be cheaters are right to be concerned about the risk of detection, and why discretion is a high priority at Ashley Madison. Mr. Biderman emphasizes that members can turn off their profiles at any time. To avoid being caught in the act of searching for—or communicating with—a corresponding candidate, users can press a panic button that pivots the screen to a movie trailer.

"Have you visited the site?" he asks.

I'm not wild about all of the aspects of the World Wide Web. It strikes me as a place where a growing number of people go to do, or think, or write bad, possibly depraved things.

"I looked at your home page, but I didn't click through," I admit. "I'm keeping myself at a safe distance from the sex."

Where there is money to be made, there will always be invention, and so it should come as no surprise that there is now software to track your partner's computer use. There are also spy phone products, which, downloaded onto your cell phone, ensure that every time your partner receives or sends an e-mail or a text on his or her cell phone, it appears on your cell phone without his or her knowing. I mention this to Mr. Biderman.

"Everything we think about is about ensuring privacy," he tells me. "Communication is kept in confidence on a secure platform. And afterward, the digital lipstick is fully eradicated."

"What do you mean by 'digital lipstick'?" I need to ask.

"Proof of illicit affairs by way of e-mail exchanges," he tells me, and then he explains that the service allows members to erase their profile information for a fee.

Technology is not my strong suit, but I've learned enough about it to understand that there is no such thing as a "secure platform," even a proprietary one. Mr. Biderman is adamant that the company's ability to protect the clandestine aspects of its service ensures "successful affairs." It does not escape my attention, however, that the very server his company has so diligently developed to guarantee discretion for the clients was collecting and tracking general data based on those clients' personal information.

"It's a relevant community to study," Mr. Biderman informs me.

I must be looking confused, because he feels the need to point out that "cheaters don't put their hands up, and affairs happen in every culture." On the off chance his point eluded me, it is repeated a third time, but in a different way: "There's nowhere on earth affairs don't happen."

WHY ANYONE WOULD offer information on his or her sexual peccadilloes with graphic bonhomie is beyond me, but I nod to Mr. Biderman so he can see that I understand. When I ask what, exactly, he is doing with the data he's collecting, his is a more deflective than explanatory response.

"Until now, infidelity has always been studied by sociologists by way of a retrospective process and from a historical perspective."

Though the anonymous data Ashley Madison is collecting is not sold, the site shares it with various parties, including universities and institutions researching marital infidelity.

"Is there a quid pro quo . . . you provide data in exchange for trending statistics that help hone your company's marketing?" I ask.

He answers rhetorically.

"If you have a chance to work with Duke University or a world-class researcher, why not take advantage of the feedback you receive in order to refine your marketing and expand your business by regionalizing it? And there's a second level of research."

"Which is?"

"We gather anonymous information volunteered from clients."

—

MARRIED PEOPLE, IT turns out, are not only interested in having sex with people not their spouses; they are willing to provide detailed information about it. I assume it has to do with participants who hail from a generation unabashed about sharing personal information online. Still, it didn't make sense. Not entirely.

"Why volunteer information you're deliberately withholding from a spouse?"

Mr. Biderman puts an unexpected spin to the point.

"Because many people having an affair believe they're morally misrepresented."

"Really?"

There was just enough condescension in my voice for Mr. Biderman to climb back on his moral high horse.

"You need to consider a different moral paradigm," he tells me. "People often turn to Ashley Madison because divorce is something they don't wish to pursue. Quite often, having an affair can save a marriage."

"Okay."

"It's a sexually cathartic experience."

"I beg your pardon?"

"Having an affair can be sexually cathartic," he repeats.

The expression on his face indicates the unlikelihood of a sense of humor; I assume he is completely serious.

Not wishing to encourage Mr. Biderman while he was busy providing me with numerous reasons he thinks he is so clever and wonderful, I say nothing. But there is a validity to one of his points: that while marriage may not always be successful if the sex in it is satisfactory, marriage has no real chance of success if the two people have completely lost their taste for each other.

"So, if having an affair can improve the chances of staying married, would you—as a businessman—consider joining the booming market in pornography on the same grounds: that a bit on the side might well benefit a marriage?" I ask.

"One-third of Internet traffic today touches adult content, but, no, we aren't in that market. On the other hand, as long as no one is breaking the law, I don't see why business should be held to someone else's idea of morality."

I suggest that volunteering information about one's sex life might be one way of offsetting guilt. Absolutely not, says Mr. Biderman. The longer we discuss the apparent willingness of Ashley Madison clients to share intimate details of their sex lives, the more I begin to agree with his point that something different is going on. Something that has to do with a cultural change within the generation of young adults who possess a different take on privacy and whose collective impulse is to share information and photographs, sometimes indiscriminately and often about and of themselves.

According to Ashley Madison's data gathered from its new customers, about 10 percent report that they have logged on to the site out of curiosity. Within three days, 80 percent change their response to "open to meeting offline." Noel Biderman insists that the site is no more responsible for a divorce than one spouse's discovery of an illicit affair. Research suggests that given the opportunity, attached men and women are almost as likely to be unfaithful. Assuming the findings are accurate, does that mean that the Internet and social media sites have evened the playing fields between men and women? I remind myself a person living in the Middle Ages was unlikely to know more than a hundred people during the course of a lifetime, and now that same approximate number of people can be scanned on your iPhone in a matter of minutes. The irreversible fact is that behavior has changed and, along with it, moral perceptions. Has technology enabled those changes, or are those changes the result of liberalized morals?

"Men have always had sexual outlets that women haven't," says Mr. Biderman.

"By that, you mean illicit affairs?"

"Yes. And that's what the Internet and our service in particular have transformed. When the algorithms kick in, it's obvious that the choices women make are a lot more liberal in the realm of an affair than in a long-term relationship. Ultimately, we are a communication platform where you gain confidence that the person you're communicating with understands what's brought you to an affair and that person is seeking the same thing you are."

Biderman claims that the core group of Ashley Madison users is between the ages of thirty and forty-five, with a fifty-fifty ratio of men to women. According to the company, women between the ages of eighteen and thirty-nine are more likely than men to be looking for illicit affairs. That reverses over the age of forty, when men are more likely to be adulterous. Ashley Madison's female clientele—regardless of age—is increasing annually, says Mr. Biderman. This coincides with recent research that attached men and women are almost as likely to be unfaithful, and so he is right to pay attention to what women want. He tells me that women respond to communication and that now "they can pursue infidelity safely and securely by building a one-on-one rapport on our site."

I have no idea what is required to establish a one-on-one rapport with someone you've not met but are, nonetheless, considering as a prospective candidate for sex. Whatever that process might be, I suspect that a woman goes about it differently than a man: that suspicion rides on my fundamental belief that there exists a lapse between men's sexual pursuits and women's expectations from sex. On the other hand, my perspective might very well be dated.

Everything changes with time, including what is expected of and denied to women when it comes to sex. In my mother's generation, women were not at liberty to have sex before they were safely married. In my generation, the number of lovers had by a single woman was a limited single digit; otherwise she might be considered "loose." That expression is now referred to as "slut shaming," a practice that has become less and less meaningful as young women become more and more equal with young men in the pursuit of sex.

Mr. Biderman excuses himself to take a phone call.

Left on my own in the Bill Clinton Room, I reflect on how it is that married members of a certain English class contain scandal by having affairs with each other. Shortly after moving to London, I was introduced to a man who, when married, had acquired the well-deserved reputation as a philanderer. He fathered children with a woman while doing the same with his wife. Adding to the moral calculation were his sub-mistresses.

THINKING ABOUT WHAT enabled this man to act on all of these things simultaneously, I could identify several common denominators: the distinctively male characteristic of compart-mentalizing; a tolerant social circle; his accepting families; and organizational skills rivaling those of an air traffic controller. He was devoutly religious, which might have been yet another enabler; forgiveness every Sunday allowed him to place marital fidelity to the side the other six days of the week.

Eventually, the man's wife quit him (not as soon as I would have guessed). He married the mother of his other children. Eventually, she also divorced him. As a single man of a certain age, he still puts his back into his affairs with the wives of other men and with younger, single women. It's the second category—the young, single women—that intrigues me. Are they emotionally naive, or is it the opposite: that they have made the coolly economic choice to shun emotional expectations in order to minister to their own sexual needs?

The latter, if I am to believe Mr. Biderman, who, having returned to the conference room, claims that a number of young, unmarried women who are logging on to Ashley Madison do so with the sole purpose of locating men for sex.

—

I AM POISED to ask Mr. Biderman if he thinks that modern women are morally free to behave like men, but he sends me in another direction when he volunteers that he's faithfully married with two young children.

The chilling smile that appears on his face makes it difficult to get an exact reading on his soul. I ask him whether his decision to remain monogamous is because he feels morally responsible toward the people who love him.

"I'm early in marriage," he says, making it sound like a warning. "I've seen the research, and what I do know is that I'll need to teach my children that there is not a single way of being married."

Agreed: all of us—in our own irksome ways—will inevitably anger and disappoint our partners. Agreed: the state of one's marriage expands and contracts in changing circumstances. Agreed: sex is the wild card in the playing deck of moral behavior. And agreed: the proposition of marriage has always been a tricky business. But as an ideal, marriage resides with sanctity and is protected by laws that denounce adultery, and though none of us operate in an entirely ethical state of being, most would agree that having an affair when your spouse is unaware is a betrayal of marital trust.

RATHER THAN ATTEMPTING to pick his way through the moral quandary of infidelity, Mr. Biderman advertises his company's facilitation of it.

Except in France.

Still standing in France is an article in the civil code written in 1804 during Napoleonic times and invoked in marriage ceremonies stipulating that married couples must show each other respect. Although France is famously known as a country of libertines, when ads by Ashley Madison featuring President François Hollande and his three predecessors were introduced reading, "What do they have in common? They should have thought of ashleymadison.com," several of the ads were removed by the police.

It is the job of language—spoken and visual—to carry messages, and moral violations to marriage reaped indignant reactions long before the French had their say. The Chinese and Japanese character for the word "safe" is

安

Actually, it's two words with a single meaning. The word "woman" sits under the word "house." The combined characters make a persuasive case for the domestic sanctity of marriage and that relevant to this enduring relationship is wisdom, reason, and decency.

The ancient Greeks must have had a similar take, for they warned mortals of avenging gods who perceived that mankind's marital violations threatened their own divine plans. Epic poems describe dire consequences of ignoring what was considered a purity of household, but those same poems weave wondrous tales of the vagrant inclinations to do just that. Though home and wife were the goals of his longing, Odysseus threw himself into globe-trotting adventures and had no problem becoming a kept man by Calypso. Here was the groundwork for allowance given men (but not women) for acts of infidelity, as long as they didn't interfere with the marriage. Difficult to ignore is that a great deal of the disruption levied against mortal men was the result of Zeus's many infidelities and that the revenge for those betrayals was sought by his wife, Hera, the goddess of marriage.

The truth is that men will be men, and women, women (whatever both mean), and no one really knows what goes on in a marriage. All of this said, I believe that the gravitational pull of a lie destroys whatever orbits around truth: decency, honor, and reciprocity—all disappear. I believe that marriage embodies a desire by two people to receive what they cannot give themselves and that the willingness to compromise is required for this to take place. I believe marriage grounds us in the here and now, and ideally it provides a predictability that doesn't deny the sexual proclivity or appetite of either spouse. More ideal still is a marriage wherein that predictability manages not to become sexual dreariness. Sometimes with words, other times without, marriage is an ongoing conversation reassuring one person that she or he can trust the person to whom she or he is married, regardless of whether a business operates to meet a shift in the moral codes or attempts to accelerate that shift in order to make a profit. I also believe that a revolving door of sexual partners in a marriage almost certainly creates unhappiness and that it is selfish to ignore that probable inevitability.

These are the things I believe about marriage. But when I am on the plane returning to London, it occurs to me that my personal beliefs about marriage—which had long ago soaked deep under my skin—are no longer applicable in the broader moral scheme of things.

The next morning—in need of information concerning a subject having nothing whatsoever to do with marriage, adultery, or sex—I hit the key for Google Search. An ad pops up on the right side of the page offering to locate someone living in my postal code interested in sex that night. Alarmed that sex was being mapped on my block—with absolutely no idea how to cope with technology that had somehow targeted me—I go to the Apple Store on Regent Street in pursuit of answers and am sent upstairs to what for those of us technologically ignorant is reassuringly called "Tech Support."

"How could this happen?" I ask the young man, trying not to stare at the ring hanging from his pierced lower lip—this being difficult because it is moving up and down as he speaks.

The issue, the young man tells me, resides with the hard drive of my laptop. Google registered the brief moment I'd logged on to the Ashley Madison site to prepare for my interview with Noel Biderman in Toronto the week before.

THE SCREEN AS A SIREN

I have a rule, and that is to never look at
somebody's face while we're having sex; because,
number one, what if I know the guy?

—*Laura Kightlinger*

Several months after Noel Biderman regaled me in Toronto with claims of Ashley Madison's impenetrable security system, reams of personal and incriminating information on Ashley Madison clients have been stolen, along with financial records and other proprietary information. Calling themselves the Impact Team, the hackers issue an online statement explaining that their decision to publish the information has to do with the alleged lies coming from Ashley Madison's parent company, Avid Life Media, when it promised its members that they were able to erase their profile information by way of a Full Delete option for a $19 fee.

There is a deadly "or else" hanging off the end of the demand that ALM take Ashley Madison off-line: "We will release all customer records, including profiles with all the customers' secret sexual fantasies and matching credit card transactions, real names and addresses, and employee documents and emails . . . [Y]ou promised secrecy but didn't deliver."

Noel Biderman and his company are being blackmailed for reasons that have remarkably little to do with the ethical issues of adultery and everything to do with Ashley Madison's charging for online security and then failing to deliver it.

The media's initial response is salacious amusement. Proving that we tend to place more importance on the privacy of those who share our values than those who do not, one radio commentator suggests that although it was immoral to breach the privacy of those Ashley Madison married clients, disclosures should be made public for anyone with a record of railing against adultery. Morality, he seems to be saying, should not be called on to protect the hypocrites.

IT'S BEEN A month since the hackers made their threat, and today they are dumping 9.7 gigabytes of stolen data that include e-mail addresses, phone numbers, encrypted passwords, log-in details, payment information, and sexual preferences. Journalists, activists, and just the plain curious are combing through the records, looking for politicians, business leaders, celebrities, and, I suspect in many cases, spouses.

Reader, we are called on to step over the ironies placed in front of us in order to acknowledge that Noel Biderman, the founder of a business that makes its money from facilitating extramarital affairs, is morally outraged by what has happened to him and his business. He refers to the "illegal action [of the Impact Team] against the individual members of Ashley Madison.com, as well as any freethinking people who choose to engage in fully lawful online activities."

In the attempt to preempt the news cycles, a number of Ashley Madison's clients take to the Internet to admit their wrongdoing. Sam Rader, a Christian blogger, is one. He produces a YouTube video explaining that his wife has forgiven him for opening an account on Ashley Madison in 2013, which he insists he didn't actually use. Never mind that a flight of imagination is required for us to believe this. In his solemn appearance—with his camera-ready wife sitting next to him—he declares that he has recouped his moral status: "I have sought forgiveness from God, and He has forgiven me."

Though Sam (I feel he would want me to call him by his first name) claims that he's been "completely cleansed of sin," others are not as successful in gaining forgiveness. Some have put their professional reputations at risk with the breathtaking stupidity of having logged on to Ashley Madison using their company e-mails. On the grim end of consequence come several reported suicides linked to the leaks, including a pastor in New Orleans. Only then does Mr. Biderman step down as chief executive "in the best interest of the company."

Though Ashley Madison denies that any of the profiles on its site are fake, the Impact Team alleges that there were six times as many men as women logging on the site. That would mean that there were tens of thousands of men hoping to meet women who were not actually there.

TO FIND THE women, I enlist Candace Bushnell, who tapped into the cultural zeitgeist of sexually liberated women during my young adulthood in the romp of pre-crash New York. *Sex and the City* debuted as her weekly newspaper column before becoming a best-selling book and reinventing itself as a hugely popular television series, reruns of which rotate endlessly on television channels in North and South America, Europe, the Middle East, and Korea. Royalties from the series—and her continued success with other projects—have endowed Ms. Bushnell with a charming cottage located in a small town in Connecticut. I return to the States to meet her there.

MS. BUSHNELL IS blond, fine boned, and expensive look- ing, even in ripped jeans. A deep-throated voice makes her words sound as if they were being lightly graveled. After a brief tour of her home and its leafy surrounds, we head to the town's center, which features a post office, a general store of sorts, a small art gallery, and a Japanese restaurant—the destination for our early lunch.

A waitress, dressed in black, seems to appear out of nowhere with menus. Ms. Bushnell chooses carefully from a selection of sushi. I order ramen. She requests sake, and I ask the waitress for a pot of green tea.

Sipping our respective drinks and eating edamame from a bowl placed equidistant between us, we discuss the current generation and how it constructs and defines itself with social media. Ms. Bushnell explains that the proliferation of sexually explicit tapes and provocative pictures shared online are ways to stake a claim on what she calls the web's psychic real estate.

"These days, everyone wants to be seen," she tells me.

"But do they need to be seen having sex?" I ask.

Without actually rolling her eyes, Ms. Bushnell, through the expression on her face, makes it fairly obvious that she was hoping I would be quicker on the uptake.

"Well, one would have to imagine that many of these things occur in the moment," suggests she. "The point I'm trying to make is that it's a way to get attention."

So am I to believe that women, posting photographs of themselves naked or having sex, are chasing after men's attention, or is it that they are performing and distributing what they believe to be the proof of their sexual empowerment?

I ask Ms. Bushnell if she thinks that technology has created a hyper-sexualized culture.

She says yes.

I ask her if she thinks men are texting things to women they would not be saying to their faces.

She says yes.

I tell her that a widely accepted psychological truth is that people are inclined to copy the actions of others in an attempt to do the "normal thing." Does she think young women are having sex without necessarily wanting to?

"Probably" is her reply.

I describe the indomitable Mary Whitehouse, who, some fifty years ago, cautioned that it was naive to equate pornography with sexual liberation, and Ms. Bushnell reminds me that the moral ground Ms. Whitehouse held was staked out before the advent of the Internet and that, even with her polemical arsenal, had Mary Whitehouse battled the same war today, she would be up against a distribution network that offers ubiquitous accessibility to pornography.

OUR FOOD ARRIVES. While I wait for my broth to cool, Ms. Bushnell wants me to consider the implications of free pornography and how it accounts for the vast number of online searches. She would like me to understand that a generation of men have come to believe that sex is supposed to look like the staged, pneumatic-like sexual performances of men with organismically ridiculous women whose body hair has been removed entirely and whose breasts have been surgically altered and that these depictions do nothing to improve the chances of mutually satisfying sex.

Zeroing in on a piece of raw tuna with her chopsticks, Ms. Bushnell tells me that she was in her twenties in the 1980s and that it was a decade of good sex for women.

"The men were more educated about women's bodies," she recounts almost wistfully. "It used to be that men had a real pride in pleasing the women."

A smile breaks through, softening her serious expression; just as quickly, a look of disappointment wafts across her face and she murmurs, "Now sex is just there," saying it more to herself than to me.

That's certainly true. Portable electronic devices provide instant access to a greater number of potential sexual partners and with the least amount of accountability. Tinder—matching some twenty-six million users every twenty-four hours—is one of the more popular location-based applications and the first to offer the user an ease of using a swiping motion to choose between photographs of other users: right swipe for a potential hookup if the person receiving the image likes what he or she sees, and left on the photograph to move on to the next one. Users see nothing but a photograph and a short tagline.

"I understand how clicking and swiping is an effective system of meeting someone," I say. "But it can also be a brutally detached method of dismissing her after having disposable sex."

I refer to "her" because my impression is that it's men rather than women setting the sexual terms of this kind of engagement.

"Am I right?" I ask Ms. Bushnell.

"Well, it does put a lot of pressure on young women to conform. If you're a young woman who's dating, and every other young woman has given a guy a blow job, it's like an audition. You're out if you don't."

The casualness of Ms. Bushnell's remark catches me off guard.

"Can you talk about that a little?"

"It has to do with how many women there are to men," she explains. "That single statistic defines the dating and mating rituals of any society. When there are more women than men, men have very little reason to make a commitment, and the women have every reason not to withhold sex."

MS. BUSHNELL IS correct: men and women design their sexual strategies based on market conditions. In China, the government has only recently abolished its one-child policy, but few can afford more than one child. A son is the equivalent of an old-age pension for his parents and is one reason why unmarried men are outnumbering unmarried women by an estimated forty million. So dire is the predicament that in some rural areas villages of bachelor men have resigned themselves to lives without wives. Their urban counterparts with disposable income advertise themselves on billboards, but for many men in the cities Camgirls act as stand-ins for the real thing.

In Western countries, Camgirls (webcam women who perform in exchange for money) typically charge a fixed fee per minute for sexual services. In China, there's the same digital opportunity, but the streaming content serves a different purpose: Camgirls (censored by China's Ministry of Culture from anything suggestive) video stream themselves going about their daily lives, and viewers can tip the streamers with virtual presents (such as a virtual hug) purchased on the same apps. Far from being sex objects, they become ersatz girlfriends to young men, who feel emotionally connected to someone on a screen, knowing, all the while, that the odds of actually having a girlfriend are stacked against them.

THOUGH A FAR less dramatic imbalance than that in China, the gender ratio tips toward men in American cities, and both sexes place male pleasure as the priority.

I tell Ms. Bushnell that there are online and mobile dating coaches, which shed some of the shame of meeting on Tinder.

"So there must be some interest in what happens after you have sex," I say. "What about the idea of relationships?"

"Here's the thing," begins Ms. Bushnell, and then stops herself, apparently having come to the conclusion that despite my professional accomplishments I remain unaware of just what it is that one sex thinks of the other.

She begins again.

"I'm sure you've talked to many men on a business level, but there's a difference between talking to men about business and talking to them about relationships. If you heard what men have to say about relationships, you'd realize that you're romanticizing them."

I look at her blank-faced.

"You need to think of men in more practical terms," she says, pointing her chopsticks at me.

IT'S TRUE THAT I bring romantic maledictions on myself by choosing sentiment over practicality. Perhaps it is for this reason that I wonder if anonymous hookups are a way to manage loneliness and why I refuse to believe that there cannot be something between men and women before, after, or despite sex. I suggest to Ms. Bushnell that in order to discover anything at all about another person, one needs context that comes only by fully engaging.

"I don't disagree," she says. "But what you're calling context is extremely difficult to find these days."

Not in Denmark.

Danes have a wider view of sex. Doctors and teachers talk openly about the pleasures that come from it, as well as the responsibilities that it requires. Young Danish women are more comfortable with their bodies than those in the same age group in different nations; young Danish men are more likely to think that sex belongs in a relationship. By the time we gather ourselves to leave the restaurant, Ms. Bushnell and I are in agreement that the Danes have managed to get sex right.

I stumble into the blinding sun. Despite the sake, Ms. Bushnell walks a perfectly straight line to the car. She drives me to my drop-off point, from which a car service returns me to New York. I board an overnight flight to London, and over the Atlantic I begin to consider the difference between love and sex.

Despite its countless renditions, sex is about taking action or not. Love, on the other hand, places us on a game board, and then, crisscrossing and backtracking, it moves us between certainty and vulnerability. Love, being preoccupied with the uniqueness of another individual, is more personal than sex and is far more treacherous; it can turn on you at any point.

What woman has not ranted about a man who's taken advantage of the benefit of the doubt she bestowed upon him? What man has not found himself in Scotch-soaked agony over a woman who's betrayed him?

Few of us have avoided the tearstained, soul-deadening despair that comes from love, so if Ms. Bushnell is correct in believing that I must be more realistic about men, I feel it only fair to be just as realistic about members of my own sex.

I decide to start with the basic proposition that women like things to be in their proper places. Not surprising, men do not always have the mind to do what women want them to do, but surprisingly often women are successful in managing men in order to get them to do precisely that, and men, for reasons they don't fully comprehend—or don't wish to admit—tend to agree to be managed by women.

THERE ARE MEN, however, aware of the codes of conduct but self-evidently unwilling or unable to live up to them. Any woman willing to throw away her mind in order to convince herself that she can bend such a man toward her agenda should be held responsible for that failed computation because, within the first few hours of being introduced, a man provides a woman all of the crucial information she needs to know about him.

So why, despite the time-tested fact there is a certain type of man dangerous for a woman to be around, would a woman allow him anywhere near?

It's quite simple really: a badly behaved man is likely to be far more fascinating and sexually alluring than a well-behaved one. He knows that seduction isn't so much about persuading a woman to do what she doesn't wish to do as about providing the right excuse for her to do what she wants.

That which feels right but is wrong is dangling bait difficult for a woman to swim past—myself included. Assiduously devoted to reason in all other matters than the heart, I fell in love with a man whose wit and charm doubled as tools to side-step the right thing to do when it made a nuisance of itself. To his credit, he never deceived me into believing that we would ever arrive at a common set of values. So deeply in love with him was I that it wasn't until I came to a mid-distance in the relationship that I realized that what had already begun was the compromising of my principles. This realization—sobering as it was—did nothing to diminish my desire for him.

That I continued to love such a morally careless man as long as I did is explained in any number of plays and novels that portray their characters as extremely attractive, even when their actions are not. Bad boys have always held great appeal.

Rakish and unrepentant trickster gods appear in every culture with the same fearless willingness to disrupt conventional morality and upend the status quo: in Navajo mythology, it is the cunning Coyote; in Australian Aboriginal mythology, the Crow is an ancestral thief who stole fire; and Chinese folklore tells of the Monkey God, who wreaked havoc in the Heavenly Kingdom, while his Nigerian counterpart, Eshu, did the same with the West African version of paradise.

Flamboyant, clever, boundless men who cause chaos have been firmly established in our literary consciousness. "Mad, bad and dangerous to know" über-cad Lord Byron was refused burial at Westminster Cathedral for his "questionable morality." And, though a fictional character, Don Juan became a byword for womanizer. Literature is littered with the badly behaved, with far more words in the English language to describe the men than the women: "rogue," "scalawag," "cad," "scoundrel," "reprobate," "ne'er-do-well." The Chinese language is without gender. In Chinese, *yi qing er bai* is the name of translucent dumplings stuffed with pork and chives; it is also the idiom for a "person of visible integrity."

We need not rely on language to know what honorable behavior looks like, and though men have been responsible for a great deal of grief and a fair share of the ridiculous, they have also been behind innumerable acts of bravery. It was a noble act when a young man, arms by his sides, stood in front of a single-file line of tanks to block their way forward in Tiananmen Square during the 1989 protests. And it was an equally extraordinary act of nobility when the driver of that first tank, under almost unbearable pressure, made the decision not to harm a vulnerable fellow human, who, standing his ground, was barring the way for the line of tanks heading toward the center of the square filled with peaceful protesters.

Few would argue that self-sacrifice in a man is the most conspicuous display of his virtue. This is why I am upset to learn what has been going on in lifeboats.

12

TESTOSTERONE: MORALITY'S ENEMY, AS WELL AS ITS HERO

Call him liar and thief; and he will only take
an action against you for libel. But call him
coward; and he will go mad with rage: he will
face death to outface that stinging truth.

—*George Bernard Shaw,* Man and Superman

By reviewing data on shipwreck survivors, Swedish economists were able to disprove the maritime code of conduct that women and children should be the first evacuated from a sinking ship. According to the head counts, it turns out that women and children had the lowest survival rate, while ships' crews and captains—having chosen the "every man for himself" approach to morality—fared best.

It doesn't make sense, I told myself, determined that it not be true. *Men have started wars and abdicated crowns for the sake of women. Why would they not ensure that women were the first on a lifeboat?*

NONE OF IT squared with what I knew of testosterone, or, more accurately, what I knew to be the implications of testosterone, some of which I witnessed in my son's development.

As a little boy with no toy guns made available, he resorted to a steel mixing bowl from the kitchen as a helmet. Clasping his small hands together—one shaped as a gun, the other used to steady it—he would go on imaginary shooting sprees after designating his closet an internment camp for the cat. It was the sheer enjoyment of his maleness that was so obviously gratifying to him. Thinking back, I realize that the enemies he imagined killing with an imaginary gun (and, at closer range, in imaginary hand-to-hand combat) were all male. Women and girls were beside the point, and so were not imagined.

Is it that men are more prone to glory than gallantry?

I won't speculate whether morality differs according to gender, but I will make room for the historical fact that where there are men, their assertion is inevitable and confrontation is likely.

Greeks and Romans shared the belief that combat should be honored; some of the most celebrated and conspicuous among their citizens were warriors. Japan ushered in the samurai and *bushidō,* a code of honorable behavior, to a degree, still rooted in the moral conduct for much of Japanese society. Landed aristocrats in Europe were, in origin, invaders. In fact, the twelfth century saw continuous warfare in Europe. There can be only so much killing before its sheer numbers require a hedge against barbarism. Italy—made anxious with the ever-increasing body count in its neighboring countries—embraced the concept of honor for the sake of self-preservation. *Scienza cavalleresca* was considered by the Italians the motivational force behind civilized and moral behavior for nobles. It was also a precursor to the chivalric code of conduct, which dictated conventions on the battlefield until its definition expanded to incorporate other aspects of behavior, including a gentleman's moral duties toward women.

A man is never too old to be humiliated by a woman. And while it is true that women bring out the best in men, they are just as capable of bringing out the worst. Also true is that women will never forgive a coward. It makes sense, then, that disputes and hostilities men endured were often on behalf of—or resulting from—women.

Dueling was one method of funneling male aggression into a socially regulated venue and allowing gentlemen to defend what they believed to be their honor and that of a woman. Rather than never-ending blood feuds, a duel was streamlined into a single, decisive encounter between two principals. Though dueling was a more measured form of violence, the number of dead in Europe resulting from it began to pile up. During the twenty-one years of Henry IV of France's reign, ten thousand gentlemen died for their honor in France. Populations were smaller then, and the aristocracy in France at the time was even smaller. By his thirtieth birthday, Chevalier d'Andrieux had killed seventy-two men before the practice was deemed a show of disrespect to the king, and so was outlawed. The royal decree could do little to discourage dueling while the king continued to issue some seven thousand pardons, almost one a day.

So destabilizing is a surplus of testosterone that every society has made a point of establishing licensed channels for the overflow of it. Today in Florence one outlet is the annual match of *calcio storico,* a centuries-old competition—less a tradition than an excuse for physical violence. Two opposing neighboring teams of twenty-seven participants play a game in a huge sandpit that calls on any and all forms of brutality to get a ball into the other team's end zone. There are no rules to speak of, no substitutions. The game ends, typically, with 20 percent of the players requiring hospitalization. I find the idea of this utterly baffling, probably because I've been denied the benefit of male glands, but it doesn't require a great deal of insight to acknowledge the link between testosterone and the many things women don't wish to do (or have the common sense not to do).

I like men. I especially like men for the wonderful ways they are different from women. I feel I must add, however, that my career has unfolded predominantly among men, and so I am not surprised to learn that studies show that men speak seventy-five percent more than woman in conference-like situations (even after taking into consideration the gender mix), and that—in the same circumstances—men interrupt women more readily than women do men. A far more egregious fault is that men have a tendency to take credit from women colleagues for an idea or suggestion when credit is rightfully due to those women. I assume this bad behavior is in the service of male ego.

I've seen how the male ego can produce staggering displays of self-delusion, and I have witnessed the full range of threat levels when it comes to male aggression. More than once as the chief of staff of an international think tank did I intervene in potentially explosive meetings among men to ensure confrontation remained at a manageable level. On one occasion, members of the Russian military apparatus and NATO representatives were having at each other so vehemently that the translators were unable to keep up. What restored something resembling order was my demand, shouted above the fray, "Gentlemen, behave!"

Women have been accused of being misled by their personal feelings, but in my various incarnations in business I've observed that men are inclined to be misled by their personal interests. Many Harvard Business School case studies read like cautionary tales of testosterone-driven decisions that have ended in abject failure, and I've witnessed enough decision making among men to believe that various ill-advised mergers and acquisitions (and, certainly, a large number of hostile takeovers) might not have occurred had it been women weighing the benefits against the risks.

An increase of testosterone among animals causes certain species to patrol larger areas for no other reason than to provoke confrontations; if that's not enough to make the leap to consider that females might be more biochemically suited than men to be better behaved, there's the issue of empathy. According to those who make it their business to study such things, the cornerstone of morality is empathy. It requires one person to take the perspective of another person. Their research suggests that on average female babies are more oriented to the faces of people, and male babies are more inquisitive about their physical surroundings. Another report indicates that, again on average, females develop a sense of empathy at an earlier age, and at a faster rate, than their male counterparts.

It's a matter of everyday observance that some men have skipped that stage of development entirely. Not long after he took me to a performance of *Macbeth,* Simon and I had drinks with one of the actors who asked why we hadn't come backstage the night we saw him onstage.

"We didn't come backstage because the performance was so awful" was Simon at his least sensitive, having already entered his gender's no-fly zone of empathy.

I don't know if I am more likely than a man to consult the facial expressions of those with whom I am having a conversation, but I assume that Simon, being male, was focused more on his surroundings than on the poor man's reaction. Attempting to haul us out of the sinkhole of silence, I redirected the conversation to Lady Macbeth's take on morality. Wasn't it interesting, I suggested, that, willing to do anything required for the grisly murder of King Duncan, Lady Macbeth called on the "spirits that tend on mortal thoughts" to give her the strength of purpose? "Unsex me here" was not so much her appeal to the spirits as an acknowledgment of what it would take to see her through the bloody deed.

AFTER HER YEARS of combat training, I would assume Jacqueline Davis has what it takes.

Ms. Davis works in what is referred to as the "security protection" business as an independent player in the extremely dangerous world of covert missions. Because she's placed herself in an almost exclusively male profession, I've invited her to lunch so that I might discover if, in her line of business, she employs different moral values from a man.

Given her line of business, it makes sense when Ms. Davis arrives at my apartment looking extremely fit. With the occupational demands of her job, her diet consists primarily of caffeine and cigarettes, and so she is delighted that I've prepared lunch.

"Do you have any faith in the morality of your fellow humans, regardless of their gender?" I ask, while ladling the soup.

"I have faith in those in my team because my life depends on it. I trust them for their skills, and I have to trust them for their moral consistency. There's no real choice in the matter."

Ms. Davis's clients have included a Russian oligarch targeted for assassination, the Saudi royal family, and Benazir Bhutto. She has been stabbed in the leg, thrown through a window, and shot at by Kashmiri snipers. Having proven to be almost unnervingly capable and courageous, she still requires a man to represent her company.

"I work in the Middle East a lot, and I look after the deputy prime minister of Iraq here in the U.K., but my fees have to be negotiated by a man," she tells me. "It's just that way."

Ms. Davis seems to thrive on opposition. In addition to performing hostage rescues in Pakistan, she has had a number of assignments in Iraq.

"There was a point I was called in because women were shooting at men, and the men didn't feel right to shoot back."

"Wait. What men?"

"Colleagues" was all she volunteers. "Every time they were coming out of the compound, they were being shot at."

I'm not following.

"You have to appreciate how Iraq worked," she tells me. "We all lived in this huge compound—the Green Zone. The

CIA did, so did MI6. And the telephone engineers, the oil engineers, the various ministers in the Iraqi government, they have close protection, supplied by private security companies from all over the world, but mostly U.K. and America. Blackwater had a lot of men there. The point is there were a lot of people out there, all with close protection, and at the time I was contacted, they were being shot at."

"By women?"

"In this case, yes, by women trained by al-Qaeda."

As I struggle to visualize what I've just been told, Ms. Davis fills in the picture with procedural details.

"You'd book your time slot for the gates to be open and for your entourage to leave the compound. But everybody has the same vehicle: white 4x4s. The guys I'd worked with had a particular time slot just before the one that the CIA had. But the CIA vehicle broke down, and the guys took the slot and drove out. First of all, women in burkas are firing at them, but then a suicide vehicle drove up beside them and kills two of the men. On the al-Qaeda website they boasted—literally twenty minutes after it happened—'We've killed two CIA officers.' They hadn't, but they thought they had."

"How had they access to the schedule to begin with?"

"Who knows? You've got the Shiites, the Sunnis, the Kurds . . . it's a tribal war, and that's the reason there will never be an integrated Iraq."

I ask her to walk me through how she handled that particular assignment.

"As soon as I arrived, I went down to the compound's entrance and asked them to open the gates. Just as I was warned, the women positioned on the outside of the gate started shooting. It didn't take long to realize that they were not actually shooting at me; they're shooting above my head."

"And . . . ?"

"I did the same, but for a different reason. I shot above their heads so I could watch them shoot at me for a while longer. Then I went back into the building and told the men that I didn't think the snipers were women.

"Why not?"

"Because they weren't moving like women," she says, and then explains that a woman's center of gravity is her hips and a man's is his chest.

"I needed proof, so the next day we barreled out of the compound in an SUV and screeched to a halt about fifty yards beyond the gate. Three of us jumped out and grabbed one of them, and it was as I thought: a sixteen-year-old boy. The reason the boys weren't hitting anyone was because, like women, they didn't have the upper-body strength to hold the guns up for very long. That was the least of it. They didn't know how to shoot, because they weren't trained. They had old weapons. They were wearing burkas, which was weird for them, and they were scared."

As Ms. Davis explained how she approached the problem, it occurred to me that her methodology was more female than male. I say this because it has been my experience that no matter what the circumstances are, women ask more questions than do men. In business, they are prone to do more due diligence, which might explain the correlation between the number of women in senior management positions and the chances of a company's breaching compliance issues. I ask Ms. Davis if she thinks that as a woman she might have perceived things differently than a man would have in the same set of circumstances she'd described.

"Absolutely. But I also know what it's like. You get hardened after three months there, and you think everyone's a complete asshole. A few things were going on: I went in with a fresh perspective, and I'm extremely observant. While the men saw a figure in a burka and with a gun, I saw head and arm movements. I saw hands on an AK-47 and thought, 'Those aren't female hands.' It's just a way of looking at things differently."

"What did you do once you'd captured the boy?"

"I sent him back out the gate in his underwear. I hate

humiliating people, but it was better for him than sending him to prison, which is what the men wanted to do."

Various studies, including one by Roger Steare utilizing his MoralDNA test, report that women, regardless of occupation, are more likely than men to make decisions based on the impact those decisions will have on others. When I ask Ms. Davis if she thinks there might be a link between testosterone and risk taking, she explains that security is less about the show of strength and more about assessing risks and minimizing them. At her company, there is something known as "Chinese Parliament." Ms. Davis works with her staff by first getting across *what* they need to achieve with any given assignment, and then she explains *how* it is she believes they can achieve it. She asks if anyone else has any other ideas.

Does she think a man would do the same under those same circumstances: asking if anyone had another idea?

"No" is her one-word answer.

"And are women less likely than men to be confrontational?"

"Yes."

Does she think that women are more likely than men to behave morally? "No," says she, "especially around money."

I would agree with Ms. Davis but with a caveat: women are less likely to cheat large numbers of people from their money because there are fewer women in positions of institutional power. What about the genetic odds of women being immoral? Are women—who, some would say, are programmed to be more nurturing than men—less prone than men toward brutality? And if that were the case, are women more likely than men to be moral creatures?

"I've met incredibly immoral women who are just as ruthless as immoral men. They just go about it differently," Ms. Davis tells me.

I suggest that because a man retains the indisputable advantage of physical strength, a woman is required to call on nonconfrontational and indirect methods with which to behave immorally. Her focus is usually limited to an individual. Typically, her success, secured in the bedroom, requires her to separate from her physical self to do what is necessary.

From what Ms. Davis shares with me, that appears to be the case with a fair number of the women connected with the Russian oligarchs and multibillionaires who hired her.

"Most of their wives have been hookers. Do you know why?"

She answers the question before I have a chance to speculate.

"Because a number of oligarchs are gay, and it's illegal in Russia to be gay, so they marry these beautiful girls as trophies."

There's nothing new about older rich men with young and beautiful women at their side, but what sounds off-kilter is the number of gay Russian oligarchs.

"How do you know that?"

"Because I've worked for enough of them."

One was a Russian-born, British media magnate holding a U.S. passport. Ms. Davis was contracted by the man's estate lawyers to protect his young son, who was the company's heir apparent, against foreign government agents from Moscow. To keep the boy from harm's way, she moved him and his mother around the world, coordinating logistics with her company's intelligence division. They rented houses when they weren't staying in hotels, often only a few nights at a time. There were private jets at their disposal, but they almost always flew commercial to hide in plain sight.

Ms. Davis moved this entourage around the globe several steps ahead of the Russian government agents until the man in question was declared dead, though it was rumored he'd been smuggled abroad to enter the U.S. witness protection program in exchange for information on his dealings with Russia's political elite. His estate lawyers agreed to pay millions to Putin, who claimed it was owed to him. The agents were called off. The boy was no longer threatened. His mother returned to

Russia with a new boyfriend. Ms. Davis had completed her assignment.

The last of the cheese and fruit that I set on the table an hour ago is all but gone, and Ms. Davis needs a cigarette.

"Besides," she tells me, "I have to go."

"How is it that you manage not to become morally jaded?" I ask as I help her with her coat.

"Oh, *I am*" is her reply.

13

IMMORAL WOMEN: OR JUST THOSE HAVING A BETTER TIME?

Being a woman is a terribly difficult task, since it consists principally in dealing with men.

—attributed to Joseph Conrad

In seventeenth-century court life, aristocratic mothers pushed their daughters in front of Louis XIV, as did dukes their wives, hoping that a successful outcome would bring life-changing riches of money and grand houses. For this reason—and in these circumstances—it was not considered immoral for women to participate in sex to the full and without remorse. This leads me to a question worth considering: When do sexual mores protect women, advance them, or impede their progress?

During my tenure at a think tank, I worked behind the scenes on issues of security and conflict resolution, and operating on the premise that engagement with an unfriendly nation was preferable to its isolation, the institute sent me deep into unknown territory. At one time, I was expected to confer with female Afghan parliamentarians, while at the same time the institute—with the intention of establishing some degree of stability in Kabul—was organizing covert discussions with a faction of the Taliban. Not surprisingly, the Taliban brought to the negotiating table draconian requirements for women.

This was a period of my career when nothing made a great deal of sense, and I put my faith in my own moral beliefs, even though they were sometimes diametrically opposed to the foreign places in which I was working. That was especially the case in the Middle East, when, at a certain point before a meeting, I was asked to wait for the other attendees in a lobby.

My eyes were cast down to my BlackBerry as I walked toward the seating area, and in the periphery what registered was the dark end of the couch on which I took a seat. It wasn't until I looked up from my BlackBerry that I realized there was a large black object positioned on that end. It was a tent of sorts, held stiff and upright by interior stays. In the tent was a motionless woman.

As a grateful visitor of foreign lands, I've been fortunate to be allowed to observe other cultures at close range. *In societies, such things are done,* I said to myself, after recognizing the fact that there was a woman housed under a tent next to me. Whether the tent subordinated the woman, only the woman would know. Of this I am sure: the tent isolated her and made face-to-face communication impossible. It is not by the outward form that we know what moral action is, but it is difficult to ignore the implications such a physical restriction might place on advancement.

Now, ten years later, to look for answers, I decide to go to Turkey.

My previous visits to Turkey were shortly before and after the country elected its president Recep Tayyip Erdogan, when he was the charismatic founder of the Justice and Development Party. Turkish colleagues and I were hopeful. Who would question the political and moral validity of the words "Justice" and "Development"?

Erdogan's early reforms went down well: he managed to establish a fragile peace with the Kurdish separatists after some thirty years of their warring against the Turkish government. But it didn't take long before his initial programs of liberalization gave way to despotic behavior, which polarized citizens, undercut the rule of law, hobbled the independence of institutions, and threatened free speech.

This time, it's not Erdogan who interests me in Turkey. I'm in Istanbul to meet Rojin.

Rojin is a pop star. She is also a Kurd. These two facts combined have created odd alliances between her and the Turkish government. A third fact, that she is a woman, threatens Turkey's political establishment that has made a point of casting her as a moral misfit.

Turkey is a place where deeply different cultures have managed to coexist for centuries. The original Indo-European underpinning of the Kurdish legacy disappeared long ago, and rather than a uniform Kurdish culture there are diverse Kurdish societies living in areas spanning the borders of Iran, Syria, and Turkey, intermixed with Arab, Armenian, Assyrian, Azeri, Jewish, Ossetian, Persian, and Turkic communities. Most inhabitants of this region are Muslim, but one of several indigenous religions practiced by the Kurds was similar to Buddhism.

Kurds, nearly 20 percent of Turkey's population, form Turkey's largest minority group, and they have posed the most serious challenge to the country's insistence on a homogeneous society. In 1999, at the encouragement of the European Union, Kurds were granted greater political power and cultural rights inside Turkey, including the freedom to speak and learn the Kurdish language.

If one thinks of modern music with ethnic roots, the name that comes to mind in Turkey is Rojin. She grew up in a multicultural household with a Syrian mother of Lebanese heritage and a Kurdish father from the Mardin province of Turkey. She sings onstage and in front of thousands of fans in Turkish, Arabic, Persian, Kurdish, and Assyrian.

—

MY MEETING WITH Rojin is at an open-air café on the European side of Istanbul, organized by mutual friends, who have also agreed to act as translators. Our table is small, and despite the serious topic we intend to discuss, the get-together takes on a festive mood. Tea is served, along with a plate of fragrant baklava.

Rojin is in her mid-thirties. When she was a student, the Turkish government didn't allow public use of spoken or written Kurdish. And when she began singing and sang in Kurdish, she was forced to appear in court for "unethical intentions." But when Turkey's president Erdogan, coveting the oil supplies in Iraqi Kurdistan, made a point of sidling up to the Kurdistan Regional Government's president, Masoud Barzani, Turkey's government went from outlawing the Kurdish language to launching a twenty-four-hour Kurdish television station.

Believing that her country's government was serious about extending the rights of Kurds, Rojin welcomed the opportunity offered to her by the Erdogan government to host a television program of her own. When, three years later the political tide turned, the government censor canceled her television program because one of her on-air cooking segments called for ingredients of lemons, peppers, and tomatoes. Their colors: yellow, green, and red—the same as the Kurdistan flag—were enough to claim that Rojin was a political agitator. When the vegetable conspiracy was not deemed damaging enough to undermine her reputation, she was labeled a "slut," the moral death knell in Kurdish culture.

In my roving life, I've worked and lived in societies that long ago decided a woman like Rojin should not exist; but one need not travel far to be exposed to the unchanged attitudes toward women. The sequence of blessings recited by traditional Jewish men at the beginning of the daily morning prayers in Borough Park, Brooklyn, includes "Blessed are you, Lord, our God, ruler of the universe who has not created me a woman." I will keep my personal thoughts to myself on this one, except to suggest that reading it out loud to your daughter is unlikely to build her self-esteem.

Here is the juncture, reader, where we might consider that women in general are not charmed by the history of their subjugation, particularly because evidence indicates that men have not been spectacularly successful in making and managing civilization. After a careful and close review of the facts, we might even arrive at the conclusion that men are often responsible for making obstacles to progress.

This declaration might cause hackles to rise, and so I shall reposition the point as something more collaborative sounding: Because important contributions to the advancement of humankind are ideas, talent, and skill, and there are no advantages in marginalizing one-half of the world's population, what is the moral purpose of casting women as inferior to men? And to the theologians, I pose the question of why religions have consistently fought against what might liberate women from those constraints.

I understand that morals are difficult to change once they are taken for granted. And I accept that the moral injustices of one sex with unwarranted advantage over the other have been maintained for centuries. I'm aware that this will not be corrected in my lifetime. But I have faith that inroads for women will continue to be made, not because I am a woman, but because I am a reasonable being, and it is a logical request of reason that we stop wasting the resources of half the members of our species with the double standard.

I ADMIRE MEMBERS of my own sex who confronted the world's small-mindedness with fierce determination and made intellectual, medical, scientific, and artistic contributions against the odds. I'm also drawn to women who—facing social stigma—decided to have a good time regardless. How could you not appreciate Lady Ellenborough, for example, a

nineteenth-century English aristocrat possessing riotous sen-
suality and unreserved confidence, who pitted herself against
the societal restrictions of conventional morality. She plowed
through four marriages, one brought to an end by an act of
Parliament after a parliamentary debate during which was
recorded, "Would anybody believe that a lady dressed to go
out to dinner could be guilty of anything improper?"

Actually, yes.

In a social world that was dressed to repress, Lady Ellenborough had a torrent of lovers, including kings, generals, and a
sheikh twenty years younger than she. But it wasn't her sexuality that invited scandal as much as her audacity. Scandal didn't
seem to bother her; whether this is an enviable trait I cannot
say, but surely one required for the unrestricted sex she had
during the course of her relatively long life.

Far from the extravagant Lady Ellenborough, who was
attracted to the theatricality of extremes and had four babies
in five years (three, illegitimate), I am still a relatively liberated member of my sex. With opportunities to support myself
financially, and access to birth control, I have been able to live
a sexual life of my choosing. But had I been living in any number of other places ruled by the non-secular, my sexuality—
deemed under those circumstances a moral atrocity—would be
the death of me, quite literally.

IF ONE WERE to consider that early history reveals a surprising lack of prudishness, it would seem odd that thousands
of years later no other aspect of human nature is as hedged
around as sex. Mystic theologies of ancient Egypt were enthusiastic hosts to sexual symbolism; religious art of Indonesia,
Africa, New Guinea, Polynesia, and South America was often
pornographic; worship sites in India and Japan adorned themselves with the explicit depiction of sex; and Babylonian and
Syrian brothels were attached to temples. I am unable to warm

to the theme of brothels and temples: I think their proximity unseemly, but my opinion concerns the issue of propriety, not of moral values.

I'm after a bigger question—one, I admit, I do not come at from a nunnery—and it is this: With such fun to be had with sex, why would humans voluntarily deny themselves the pleasure? I suspect that much like the moral codes that keep us in line, the regulation of sex has to do with control.

There is no prize in guessing which gender was controlling and which was being controlled. Men wrote the Bible, and the Bible cannot be confused with a charter for women's rights. Eve, believed by many to be the first woman, is portrayed as a temptress and was designated as the responsible party that made sex and sin one and the same.

BECAUSE SEX WAS deemed a sin, the scriptures insisted that Mary conceive as a virgin. When the church instructed that sex defiled the religious spirit, it felt compelled to remove the slightest taint of sex by determining that Mary remain a virgin after giving birth. Still not satisfied, it ordained that purity reach back not just one generation but two: Mary's image was returned to the dry cleaner yet again, this time in the second century, when scriptures were rewritten to convey that Mary was herself conceived without sin.

It wasn't enough that the church identified marriage as a refuge for sin ("But if they cannot exercise self-control, they should marry. For it is better to marry than to burn with passion."—1 Corinthians), the church forced itself into the marital bedroom. Pronouncements were made on what could and shouldn't be done between the sheets. Celibate priests and monks—themselves denied sex—turned their attention to anyone else having it. Rules were devised for sex. Break the rules and go to confession, where penance provided absolution. It was a brilliant strategy: by transforming sex—the most potent impulse of living beings—into guilt, the church set the moral agenda for sex.

THERE IS PERHAPS no Western nation with a more contradictory approach to sexual taboo than America, where, lo and behold, the mind-bogglingly popular erotic romance novel *Fifty Shades of Grey*, notable for its explicitly erotic scenes of the give-and-take between bondage and discipline (I speak not of the kind of discipline required to conjugate Latin), sold extremely well in the Bible Belt, where morality is rooted in the politically and culturally conservative southern states. That is not the outcome one would have predicted.

A movie was made from the book. Its record-breaking box office sales were due, in some part, to the marketing strategy linking the taboo subject to mainstream entertainment, and any lingering stigma was scrubbed when the two stars were featured on the cover of the mass-market-friendly magazine *Entertainment Weekly*. To position the product at a safe distance from whatever moral condemnation there might have been, the movie was advertised on television during the Super Bowl, and it opened to the public on Valentine's Day. But this kind of brick-and-mortar marketing of sex is not what has made an evolutionary impact on modern Western sexual mores and, to a profound degree, its morals. The change agent for sex is the Internet and a proliferation of its foot soldiers, mobile devices.

IN A QUIET, semirural community in Colorado, confusion ran riot among parents and the district attorney's office when it was discovered at its high school that at least a hundred students—and some eighth graders from the middle school— were swapping naked pictures of themselves. Boys and girls— some as young as twelve—were involved in equal numbers, leaving law authorities to debate whether to file child pornography charges in light of the fact that the felonious charges would be brought against participants who were themselves under age.

Morality, it seems, is up for grabs in America's heartland.

PART FOUR

*Taking the Bother
out of Morality*

CELEBRITIES AS STANDARD-BEARERS

Hi. I'm Richard Gere, and I'm
speaking for the entire world.

—televised message broadcast in Palestine in
advance of its 2009 presidential elections

Difficult to believe, but nonetheless true: Richard Gere was—
and perhaps still is—under the impression that he speaks to
Palestine for "the entire world."

In a similar, mirrored embrace of fame, the supermodel
Naomi Campbell, after being sentenced for abusing her maid,
insisted she was unable to surrender her passport because she
had an appointment to visit Nelson Mandela of South Africa.
Celebrities have increasingly exerted political pressure by back-
ing national causes and by leveraging their fame in an attempt
to shape policy—often in someone else's country. More than
that, they feel they must teach the rest of us.

To understand why very rich actors and performers feel entitled to scold us about climate change, racism, sexism and sexual
abuse, and corporate greed, I invite Alison Jackson to breakfast.

MS. JACKSON IS a multifaceted artist living in London who
takes photographs, makes films, produces television programs,

creates advertising, and packages books; all of these endeavors concern our fixation with celebrities. By staging scenes with look-alike celebrities, she is able to mimic the power of the celebrity culture successfully and simultaneously explore the public's expectation of it. Satirizing politicians, royals, and celebrities by portraying their imagined private lives in grainy photographs, she has depicted Robert De Niro surrounded by half-naked call girls, as well as the queen reading a dog magazine featuring corgis while sitting on the toilet, lacy silk underwear around her ankles.

It has been suggested that we meet at the Wolseley, a European-style café-restaurant on Piccadilly next to the Ritz hotel, but the day before, when I phone the restaurant to make a breakfast reservation, I am informed that the earliest a table would be available is the afternoon. Because afternoon is not when breakfast usually occurs, I redirect Ms. Jackson to the Arts Club, a few short blocks away.

I have arrived before she does to claim a comfortable booth. A moment later, she is striding toward me, looking every bit the contemporary artist—black leggings, black biker jacket, black boots—and clutching an iPad. The waiter appears and is informed that we both are in need of something caffeinated as soon as possible.

I BEGIN BY asking how her interest in celebrities came about.

"The way the celebrity magazines work is that the more pictures you see of these celebrities, the more you think you know them, but you don't know them, and the more you want to know them more. What fascinates me is that what you think is real isn't. With the mass bombardment with imagery, it makes it very easy to tell untruths, and we know facts only through the media, because we can never know the real people. I was exploring, at the time, the hyperbole of the icons and the importance of celebrities in our lives. How they enter our collective psyche. I'm not interested in the celebrities themselves, but the perception of the celebrity. And how, more and more, we read our information through imagery, which is an extremely fast way of getting information."

Ms. Jackson was initially criticized for the images she staged (one image in particular appeared at the outbreak of the war in Iraq, picturing a President George W. Bush look-alike reading the Koran upside down), but as her artistic appeal grew, her onetime critics invited her to stage pictorial spreads in their publications that featured faux celebrities. Her exploration of celebrity had come full circle.

Ms. Jackson explains that the web has allowed the dissemination of an endless number of images of celebrities and that by using the screen, Kim Kardashian has actualized the concept of celebrity.

"I'm almost sure there is a third party in the room filming it."

"Filming what?" I ask.

"The sex tape. It was a blow job."

Undisguised discomfort crosses my face.

"So I guess you haven't seen the tape."

Ms. Jackson is referring to Kim Kardashian's sex tape with the singer Ray J, which appeared online.

"What makes you think it might have been filmed by a third party?"

"Because it was a business decision."

"A business decision? What kind?"

"You need to speak to her mother, Kris. She's behind it all."

"Including the camera?"

Ms. Jackson's expression lights up by what she now believes was possibly true.

"She might very well have been the third person in the room, which would make her the one filming her daughter's sex tape."

Kris is Kim's mother and manager, and according to Ms.

Jackson she's masterminded the Kardashian empire of reality programming, which features a predominantly female family attired in Lycra and see-through mesh. Kim is married to the co-celebrity, man for all seasons Kanye Omari West, a rapper also known as a hip-hop record producer, fashion designer, and entrepreneur. Kim and Kanye are parents of a boy, Saint (I kid you not), and a girl, North West (really).

"Without her mother at the helm, none of them would be as famous as they are today. I'm sure she was behind Caitlyn's marketing," Ms. Jackson tells me.

For those unaware—and there must be very few—Caitlyn Jenner was formerly known as the Olympic gold medal winner Bruce Jenner, who, while married to Kris, was Kim's stepfather. The entire family appeared worldwide on the reality program *Keeping Up with the Kardashians*. This was before Bruce's gender reassignment. If you are trying to sort out why Bruce's decision to change himself from a man into a woman would unfold so publicly, you are not keeping up. The point here is that Bruce becoming Caitlyn was enough to transform her into another, different, self-promotional television personality who would star in her own reality show, *I Am Cait*.

Ms. Jackson wants me to understand that this kind of celebrity brand building is first about recognizing the opportunity and then about controlling the images. We discuss the *aren't I fabulous,* three-quarter portrait of Caitlyn Jenner on the cover of *Vanity Fair* magazine, which launched her coming-out campaign. She was pictured in a bathing suit, and the photograph was cropped deliberately to show us that she'd gone from man to woman in every sense. I suggest that no woman Caitlyn's age of sixty-five—regardless of retouch—would have agreed to appear on the cover of a magazine pictured in a bathing suit, and that the point being made was located in her genital area.

"Absolutely right," enthuses Ms. Jackson. "And it worked, didn't it?"

"I'm not sure what is meant by it working," I say. "But that's certainly where my eyes went first."

"It's choosing the one image that will instigate our voyeurism" is how Ms. Jackson explains it.

A second round of coffee enables us into more conversation. We discuss how images have overtaken the written word as the catalyst for moral change. I mention Jan Morris, born James and with whom I had the privilege to work at one time. A superlative writer of history, social commentary, and travel, her 1974 autobiography, *Conundrum,* told of her journey in 1972 to Morocco where James became Jan. Beyond that, she felt no reason to explain.

"But Jan Morris had no need to market herself," Ms. Jackson says. "And marketing is all there is with the Kardashians because you can't just give a blow job and then get a TV series."

MS. JACKSON CONTINUES her point.

"Kim's sex tape would have been just another blow job pictured on the Internet had it not been for a strategic idea behind it, and the business acumen to successfully implement a brand-building campaign. First, you have to control the image; and then you have to know how and when to leverage it."

I am given a brief history lesson of the screen, beginning with the Hollywood stars in the 1950s.

"The studios chose a limited number of big stars," explains Ms. Jackson. "The public relations photographs were very glamorous shots that the public could admire. Then television came along, and there were television stars, not as big as movie stars, but stars nonetheless. The next distribution vehicle was the Internet. Kim Kardashian belongs to the newest distribution outlet, which is social media. If you want to brand anything today, it's about social media marketing. The image is paramount today," repeats Ms. Jackson. "If you construct imagery in the right way, those looking at the image can't get it out of their psyche, and when that image goes into the collective psyche, you've built an icon—something that can be branded. You should read Jean Baudrillard's commentary on consumerism," she tells me. "He was a French sociologist but also a photographer, and he wrote about how different objects are consumed in different ways and that needs are constructed, rather than innate."

We discuss how the instantaneous and frenzied postings on social media of almost all aspects of a celebrity's life enable the brand to effectively endorse a wide variety of products.

"Marketing yourself successfully gives you the opportunity to make a great deal of money endorsing other brands," says Ms. Jackson. "David Beckham will sit in a studio and manufacture four different looks—gay icon, good father, great footballer, aging but sexy guy—and he can distribute each depending upon what is needed to be sold, to whom, and where."

"David Beckham has a well-earned reputation as a football player," I point out. "Many others who become celebrities are without skill or talent."

"It almost doesn't matter. Look, I'll show you something," Ms. Jackson says, reaching for her iPad so that I can watch a video.

The video shows bedlam in a shopping mall in Japan where Angelina Jolie and Brad Pitt are being protected by security. Surrounding them is a squealing crowd of young Japanese jostling for a spot to take pictures on their iPhones and tablets.

The thing is, it's not Angelina Jolie and Brad Pitt but look-alikes created by Ms. Jackson and her studio assistants.

"Everyone knew these were not the real Angelina Jolie and Brad Pitt," says Ms. Jackson. "The same thing happened when we took Beckham look-alikes to Madrid."

According to Ms. Jackson, some members of the public end up hounding a celebrity look-alike to have sex with him or her.

"I can see that being in close proximity to celebrities is seen as a sign of status," I tell her. "But what possible value is there when it comes to someone who *looks like* someone famous?"

"It's the image."

"But the image is false."

"It doesn't matter. They think that it's going to rub off on them in some way. What you can't have, you're desperate for, and you greedily try to run after it. It goes from being the subject to the object."

I am unable to fathom Ms. Jackson's disclosure, yet its underlying premise depresses me. Does she think that the celebrity culture has altered morality; is it, in fact, a moral matter?

"I think celebrity is like a new religion of mini-saints and each celebrity represents a different saintly quality. But we never really know that saint, even though we are living at the same time he or she is, because everything about them is curated or edited . . . everything about them incites voyeurism. And because so much today resides on the surface, it is easier to lie. And because it is easier to lie, it is easier to lose your integrity."

AFTER BREAKFAST WITH Ms. Jackson, and in the hope of putting modern-day celebrity in historical context, I head to the library for Jean Baudrillard's *Consumer Society,* the book she has suggested. But once I begin to browse the stacks, it's Chaucer's *House of Fame* I decide to read. Composed of two thousand lines written in couplets, the poem recounts a dream sequence in which Chaucer tells of his journey to a glass temple, located at the spot where land, sea, and sky converge. The temple is built on a massive rock made of ice, and its base is etched with the names of the famous, many of which have melted to the point of being illegible. Entering the glass temple, Chaucer sees that it is filled with singers whose songs convey the stories of mortals longing for fame. Courtiers rush back and forth. On a dais, in the center of this frenzied activity, is Fame herself. Around Fame's throne swirl petitioners seeking her favor to no avail.

Modern technology has given the concept of fame an increasing number of outlets. When Kim Kardashian appeared on the cover of *Paper* magazine in 2014, her bare and oiled-up buttocks were featured above the caption "Break the Internet." *Paper*'s website received 15.9 million views that day (compared with the average daily views of 25,000). A year later, *Forbes* reported Ms. Kardashian to be the highest-paid reality star, with annual earnings of almost $53 million, adding that she "monetized fame better than any other." Her recent video game made $80 million, and her prodigious output of self-regarding content included a 450-glossy-page collection of photographs in a book—published by Rizzoli no less—titled *Selfish,* wherein she describes the series of self-portraits as "a candid tribute to my fans."

There she is, in all of her relentless wonderfulness, assisted by the $200,000 spent annually for her makeup. Reality television star, Internet diva, endorser of products, author, and global selfie subject—lest we forget just how this treasure trove of talent first made itself known, it all began with someone taping her with a penis in her mouth.

Not so many years ago, it was safe to assume that the public release of a sex tape would result in embarrassment. At its possible worst, it would threaten both family and career. A sex tape today, if astutely handled, can become an asset.

In a time when sex has emerged as a major focus of consumerism, the Kardashian women have an innate understanding of the value that comes from combining content with marketing. Dealing with her own sex tape with a mastery of social media, Kim Kardashian has harnessed whatever criticism there may be into furthering her moneymaker brand. With quotidian triviality and no detail of her life deemed insignificant, she is controlling her narrative—and thus her brand—by showing more and more of herself.

Declaring that as long as the public thinks she looks great and her husband doesn't mind (her children are conveniently too young to ask), Kim has no problem taking a picture of herself naked and posting it for a fee. She says that she will continue to share her sexual empowerment with her legions of young fans (some forty-one million on her Twitter account alone), monetizing that shared experience in as many ways as there are to distribute it.

"I will not live my life dictated by the issues you have with my sexuality. You be you and let me be me" is the proud declaration that appears on Ms. Kardashian's personal app, which has a $2.99 per month access fee.

REALITY REDEFINED

Let be be finale of seem.

—from Wallace Stevens's poem "The Emperor of Ice-Cream"

My year of contemplating morality is passing me by while I am stuck on issues of sexual mores, specifically, how it is that fellatio is now considered less a sexual act and more a method of improving the chances at a relationship.

I decide that what is needed is a dispatch report from the front lines.

"It's not considered sex," I'm told by a woman in her early twenties, who doesn't seem to expect anything from the men in return.

"When did having a penis in your mouth stop being considered sex?" I ask another woman, closer to my age.

"When Bill Clinton told us so" is her reply.

"I DID NOT have sexual relations with that woman"—that woman being a twenty-four-year-old White House intern, Monica Lewinsky—insisted the then fifty-one-year-old president Clinton—with his wife, Hillary, at his side. His forceful denial was issued at a press conference: looking straight at the camera, he told the world that it wasn't sex he had.

If Ms. Lewinsky's semen-stained blue dress could talk, it would beg to differ. Fellatio is a sexual encounter. The owner of the dress had a sexual encounter with the president. I suppose the question is how many sexual encounters does it take to get to the term "sexual relationship"?

Twenty years after Bill Clinton's scandal, we are living with devices and websites that have become extensions of our physical selves, which is why my mind returns to Toronto and the question I asked Noel Biderman several months ago: Has technology encouraged us to behave in ways we would not otherwise?

I don't have an answer quite yet. But on the immediate front, what is mystifying me is why a man would agree to have sex with himself online (I'm using as nice a way of putting it as I can), because, according to today's newspaper, that is precisely what's happened. The young man in question was targeted by a woman on Facebook who first sent him "friend" requests and then suggested that he perform explicit acts on Skype's online video service. After sending her videos of the various encounters he had with his private parts, the woman threatened to publish the videos unless he agreed to pay her not to.

An online blackmail scheme is just that: a scheme that has been executed online. What interests me more is the web-based rendition of "hell hath no fury like a woman scorned" called "revenge porn," now against the law in the U.K. Currently being considered by the courts is a case concerning the consensual videotaping of a well-known actor and his then partner having sex. After the pair split, the woman created a fake Facebook profile and uploaded explicit pictures from the video to the man's own Facebook page. This is extremely bad behavior on the part of the woman.

It would be foolish to conclude that technology is to blame for the stupidity of the man or the immorality of the woman, just as it would be unreasonable to assume that the decision to commit adultery is a result of logging on to Ashley Madison. But in the case of Ashley Madison, the technology that enabled online cruising made adultery a great deal easier. And so it seems to me that, yes, the technology Ashley Madison promised and then made available to its clients might very well have steered behavior, encouraging men and women to act in ways they would not otherwise.

IF THE INFORMATION gathered from its leaked database is accurate, Ashley Madison often placed men in delusional cul-de-sacs by creating tens of thousands of profiles of nonexistent women. It accomplished this with software called fembots, which brought an army of fictitious women to life by animating them with the ability to send chat messages and e-mails to men (real ones) signing on to the Ashley Madison site.

It's one thing to be a victim of your own self-blindness and stupidity by being lured into a scheme by nonexistent women you assume are real, another thing entirely when you've chosen to share yourself with some other thing you know is pretending to be real. Microsoft introduced Chatbot, a computer operating system of artificial intelligence designed to simulate conversation with one or several humans on their smart phones via audio or text. It did this by keeping track of the user's personal details and regularly inquiring how he or she was feeling about a previously mentioned incident in a prior conversation. Though it needed refining (Microsoft was forced to silence the program after the algorithm found its way to the dark side and began making racist comments and sexual suggestions online), Chatbot will no doubt reappear in a more regulated guise, and for that reason I am curious if its kind of technology means that the architecture of morality will increasingly be built with ersatz—rather than real—human interactions. Various people in London refer me to Jane Buckingham, the L.A.-based founder and president of a firm that utilizes digital technologies to forecast societal trends.

"It used to be that young people had a limited number of

ways to present themselves to their friends," she tells me when I phone her. "Today, they've been liberated by technology to be whoever or whatever they want. The Internet, in particular, offers them an 'elastic self.' "

Increasingly, the way young people think of themselves goes hand-in-hand with how they display their lives online. They are deft networkers who possess a canny social media strategy and are savvy about the visual language of presentation—enough so to take into account the time of day they should post a picture in order to maximize the number of likes it gets.

Ms. Buckingham lists the current social platforms: Facebook, available to those you invite, where one creates a kind of idealized, pictorial story of one's life; Instagram, which everyone can see and is carefully curated; Snapchat, less likely to be viewed by parents; and Finstagram, a kind of fake Instagram account that allows you to be your real self.

"So the chance to be real is with the opportunity to be fake," I say glibly.

MS. BUCKINGHAM, HEARING the condemnation in my voice, suggests that it is unworldly of me to dismiss all of this as vacuous or to assign a lesser moral capacity to the current generation because they've grown up more on-screen than off. She tells me that I'm making a mistake to assume that communicating from behind the screen leads to isolation and detachment. And she reminds me that the current generation enjoys online communities and bulletin boards that generate relationships that would not have occurred had it not been for technology.

All true. But that same technology often creates a digital reality where prejudices are able to spread across smart phones and laptops. Facebook, possibly the most visited website in the world with 1.65 billion people using the service every month, provides an estimated 70 percent of them a chosen gateway to reading news. As long as it is allowed to identify itself as a platform rather than a publisher, it is able to abdicate responsibility for its content, which is likely slanted one way or another. Even if news appears on Facebook by way of algorithms alone, it is wise to remember that algorithms are programmed to make decisions, and so there is probably someone at Facebook making decisions about which decisions.

Twitter offers some 310 million monthly active users the opportunity to enthuse endorsements or hurl insults 140 characters at a time with no need to see or hear the effect either has on the receiving end.

Phones, as well, have changed the manner in which we communicate, for they have become less about speaking to one another than about sending text messages. Deloitte, the professional service firm, reports that more than a quarter of smart-phone users use their mobile phones not to make phone calls but to text, and assuming the trend continues, there will be very few smart-phone users left talking by 2020. Talking is being usurped by texting, removing yet more of the emotional nuance of human communication.

I wonder if any or all of this will have an impact on morality, and so I look for a scientific perspective to balance the sociological one I've received from Ms. Buckingham.

THE WEB WONDERS WHAT'S SO
GREAT ABOUT THE TRUTH

What we do belongs to what we are; and
what we are is what becomes of us.

—*attributed to Henry Van Dyke, nineteenth-century*
American author, educator, and clergyman

Holding thirty-two honorary degrees from British and foreign universities and brandishing a repository of data, clearly delineated arguments, and a stern determination, Baroness Susan Greenfield is a research scientist who has studied how screen technologies such as computer games and social media may be changing the human brain: more specifically, how these environments may alter (a) how we process information, (b) the degree to which we take risks, (c) how we socialize, and (d) how we view ourselves. She has published a wide range of books on the mind and the brain; she has also co-founded a biotech company developing a novel approach to neurodegenerative disorders. These accomplishments have been duly acknowledged by a nonpolitical life peerage and L'Ordre National de la Légion d'Honneur.

Due to Baroness Greenfield's busy schedule, she and I are unable to meet. Coordinating dates and times with her assistant, I choose the phone call option over a possible Skype conversation because I feel more myself off a screen than pictured on one—a testament to the generational differences we are likely to discuss.

Nine hours a day of media is not an unusual amount for someone of the current generation. So what happens when he or she looks up from the screen to interact with the world? One of Baroness Greenfield's areas of research has to do with the young brain and, because the young brain is so impressionable to the environment, how the new and unprecedented environment of the cyber world might affect it. I am hopeless when it comes to science, but in anticipation of our call I read what I can understand about the frontal lobes of the brain, the most recently evolved part of our brains, which enable us to think spatially, to make plans, and to put those plans in motion. The development of the frontal lobes becomes a constraining influence over our urges, which might otherwise overwhelm common sense, and explains why young children, no matter how intelligent, have a tendency to do the first thing that occurs to them. As you get older, there are preexisting connections in your brain that form a basis for you to have an evaluative judgment as to what is happening. In other words, you assess your thoughts against the checks and balances of the connections that already exist, and at the same time that ongoing experience updates and upgrades the existing connections, so your brain is in this fabulous dialogue with every experience you have with the outside world.

Baroness Greenfield believes that if and when this very sensitive, vulnerable, and impressionable brain function develops primarily in an environment limited to two dimensions—offering only two senses, sound and vision—the brain begins to change because that's what it's evolved to do. Quick to suggest that she's not advocating an opinion on whether these changes will be good or bad, simply that they will occur, she points out that the use of electronic devices is woven into modern childhood, with some children given tablets as early as two years old. Emphasizing, again, that she doesn't have a single hypothesis as to whether growing up with so much screen time is good or bad, Baroness Greenfield tells me that the press often misquotes her, mangling her message into a sensationalized warning that technology will harm the brain. The *Guardian*, for example, ran an article about her with the headline "Susan Greenfield and the Rise of the Facebook Zombies" and posed the question of what was more dangerous: technology changing our brains, or scientists (presumably like Susan Greenfield) who were mutating into priests.

I MUST TELL you that the woman didn't give any signs over the phone that she is dangerously mutating from one thing to the other. Quite the opposite: she indicated to me that she continues to reflect seriously on the long-term issues of technology and the brain. I, on the other hand, have no need to reflect very long before concluding that the Internet is not necessarily on a quest to advance measured intelligence. As someone who has spent a great deal of her career in business, I am leery of its altruistic promise to democratize the world. The economics of the Internet are driven by financials and dominated by very few, very profitable tech giants whose first order of business is to create profit and to increase the market's perception of share value. Technology—advanced by man's drive and its profitability—will continue to push ahead. The question is, will it change our moral selves, and if so, how and to what?

"Although these technologies seem entrenched as part of our culture, they've only been with us for ten years or so," Baroness Greenfield points out. "The generation that's going to be the most affected are the teenagers today, so, at the moment it's really hard to make predictions. Nonetheless, there might be issues concerning empathy."

She explains the neurological tools that enable us to remain moral. Self-control is one: it is morality's taskmaster. Another is empathy. Empathy—how to treat people—facilitates compassion and thus improves the chances of moral behavior.

Self-control is an acquired skill. So, too, is empathy. Neither is likely to develop by interacting on-screen.

I make the observation that the screen can give an impression of empathy without requiring proof in any applicable way. When, for example, a website reporting a disaster includes the icon of a candle, one need only click the icon to be given the impression of contributing to a larger good.

Baroness Greenfield and I discuss the implications of a click that produces no meaningful contribution but allows the person to believe that it has made him or her a better person. Some say that slacktivism, a trend within Western social media, is the result of the two-dimensional expression of global empathy it offers. So is technology, by removing us from the actuality of what empathy might demand of us, inhibiting our emotional range, or does it simply amplify human nature?

"Both those things," says she.

I'm critical of the Internet as a rolling invitation to nurse grievances, which, to my mind, leads to an erosion of critical thinking skills. At its worst, it encourages ugly cyber bullying and trolling.

Baroness Greenfield points out that there has been, and always will be, a playground bully but she agrees that technology might be producing an inability to negotiate aggressive and unwarranted human behavior.

"There are aspects of body language and interpersonal communication skills that are our tools to offsetting the bad behavior of others. This is the first time that the hand brake has been removed, and a scenario has been allowed for something that has been part of human nature to flourish unfettered. It's not as though humans were never cruel and spiteful before; it's that the screen removes the tactile intimacy of human contact, creating a kind of perfect storm that enhances those tendencies . . . tendencies that might otherwise have been held in check."

It seems to me the way screen technology consumes and is consumed doesn't foster considered debates as much as it rewards muddled ideas and the expression of our worst selves. Though there is no direct evidence that social media has shaped the way we look at ourselves and view the wider world, no one can argue the fact that it influences the way we are expressing ourselves. I ask Baroness Greenfield if the short and very personal comments freely given are the reason so many people sound so angry online.

"I think that's right," she says. "Normally, when we speak, we look the person we're addressing in the eye, we hear the tone of their voice, and we can use hand gestures, and of course there is body language. Words have just about ten percent of the impact when interacting with another person. With only words at your disposal, you are more likely to express yourself in extreme terms."

My conversation with Baroness Greenfield prompts me to consider morality in the virtual reality of video games. But because the English in particular and the Europeans in general don't appear enthusiastic about anything too virtual, to find out if assimilating into a virtual world on-screen disconnects one from so-called real-world morality, I return to New York in February—its least lovely month—to meet Eric Zimmerman, considered the Lou Reed of web and non-web games.

Mr. Zimmerman was co-founder and chief design officer at GameLab, a game development company based in New York City. Recently, he and Nathalie Pozzi, an Italian architect and principal of an interdisciplinary design studio, also based in New York, have designed a series of large-scale game installations. Their collaborations have appeared at events and exhibitions at New York's Museum of Modern Art and the Smithsonian American Art Museum, as well as in Paris, Dublin, Moscow, and Los Angeles. In addition to being a game designer, Mr. Zimmerman is a founding faculty member at NYU's Game Center, which is its own discipline within the university's Tisch School of the Arts and located in Brooklyn, a place where sleek, multimillion-dollar condominiums have begun to poke up from the grainy surface.

Mr. Zimmerman meets me at the elevator banks on his floor of a building that gives the impression of something less arty and more corporate than I expected. He is wearing a T-shirt, jeans, and stylishly large, black-rimmed glasses.

His office features an outsize computer and a large bulletin board with what looks to be a step-by-step narrative for a game. A few brief moments into our conversation is all it takes for him to realize that mine is a severely limited technological reach.

"It might be helpful if we were to start with some basic statistics" is his diplomatic suggestion.

"Ninety-seven percent of American teenage girls play digital games of one sort or another; ninety-nine percent of boys," Mr. Zimmerman tells me. "Games have become increasingly like music. You don't ask, 'Do you listen to music?' You ask, 'What kind of music do you listen to?'"

He explains that games now feature suit yourself sexual identities: pansexual, transsexual, bisexual. This interests me. Sex—no matter how much imagination is applied on its behalf—has remained unchanged as long as it's been around. But sexuality is another issue, and it's obvious from what I've learned these past several months that the current generation has managed to bring something new to sexuality by insisting on an adaptable definition of it. I tell Mr. Zimmerman about my conversation with Jane Buckingham the previous month and say that when I asked her if an increased number of culturally endorsed sexual choices for this current generation was (a) confusing, (b) an opportunity, or (c) a style statement, she replied that based on her company's focus groups, it is more (b) and (c) than (a). Mr. Zimmerman can see how the increased number of gender-related ways to identify oneself isn't confusing, how it means simply that there are more options and available opportunities for sexual identity. To that point, Game Center had just hosted a conference called "Different Games," specifically focused on game creators who are transgender or gay and how new games relate to who they are. It also hosts an annual event for fighting games, which draws a very different crowd that is, nonetheless, extremely diverse in terms of ethnicity.

Mr. Zimmerman speaks convincingly of how playing games is universal in human culture and how the rise of digital technology has given games a renewed relevance.

"You play a game for no other reason than the pleasure of interaction. There is no end outside the invitation to play."

I ask him if he designs games that put the user in front of a moral decision.

"In design classes, we talk about ethical issues quite a bit. Designers have an absolute imperative that what they're doing when they create a world on-screen is fitting within the larger cultural landscape. I expect my students to take responsibility for the kinds of representations they feature in the games they design and the situations they put their users in. I think there are some specific and interesting connections between games and ethics and morality. I would say that every game is itself an ethical laboratory."

Mr. Zimmerman directs my attention to what he calls the Magic Circle, a concept in digital media that refers to the membrane that encloses a space apart from ordinary life where different rules apply. I ask if the moral tenets of how to behave in the Magic Circle are the same as in the world outside it, even when the game invites you to kill opponents as a form of entertainment.

"Yes and no," Mr. Zimmerman says. "You and I might be friends, but within the temporary Magic Circle that is in place while we are playing, you are my adversary. So I will do whatever is needed to defeat you. You might ask me what am I going to do next, and I might lie to you. Games often let us do something taboo . . . something that violates a social moral rule. But we're doing this in a stylized representation, and we're giving each other permission to do things we would not be doing outside the circle, because play is always voluntary."

I make no comment, and so we conclude with Mr. Zimmerman calling on the full range of his tact to tell me that it was a pleasure to have been given the chance to converse with "someone like" me. It's fairly obvious that he realizes that I'm a lost cause—in and out of the Magic Circle.

I can do nothing about my limited self in the sphere of virtual worlds, but mulling over my next moral topic—drone attacks—I try to imagine what happens when the Magic Circle's objective is to kill a real person by remote video control, in a way that is legally and morally sanctioned by your government.

17

ETHICALLY SANITIZED WARFARE

It is forbidden to kill; therefore, all murderers
are punished unless they kill in large numbers
and to the sound of trumpets.

—*Voltaire*

A drone attack is eerily silent.

I've seen a tape. An aerial view shows four people walking down the road. There's a quick, short flash. Something shoots off to one side—a head. The three-dimensional images collapse into a flat orange stain that bleeds out to the edge of the frame. When it clears, there are no more people.

Several things were expected of me as I was watching the tape. I was expected to believe that the four people were killed because, while they lived, they were a viable threat to the United States. Expected from me as well while watching the tape was that I put my trust in the sanctioned review process that targeted the four people—a process with very little oversight and composed of a select number in the U.S. military establishment. I was also to take for granted that the four people killed were the right four people (if "right" is the word) and that no one of them was someone else.

—

A DRONE CAN identify a target with more precision than ground troops or a conventional pilot. Drone operatives, whose locations are thousands of safe miles away from their strike, are able to hover over or track a target days in advance of the strike. Once launched, the missile can be diverted from its original target in an intentional miss before impact.

More difficult to verify are the other facts, including varying casualty reports. While officials insist that drone strikes result in only incidental collateral damage (a morally sanitized way of saying that innocent civilians are killed), that claim is difficult to confirm, hampered by the secrecy of the strikes. Human Rights Watch estimates that upward of twenty-six hundred people have been killed by drone attacks, while the empirical evidence suggests that drones—because of their precision—result in fewer civilian deaths than manned strikes.

The idea of using drones to kill individual enemies, specifically in the sovereign territories of other nations, is a dangerous principle to cede. If a Pakistani family is wiped out, along with the entire wedding party as a result of the unlikely but fatal mistake of a drone attack, to whom or what does one turn? Was the mistake committed in Pakistan where the bomb landed, in the airspace from which it was launched, or in the air-conditioned bunker located somewhere in America?

THE USE OF technologically advanced and unmanned weaponry divides almost immediately into two camps: one insisting that remote control makes killing and destruction too easy and is therefore less moral; the other camp insisting that there is nothing new about launching a strike from a distance. This point is meant to resonate with the example of the Hundred Years' War between the English and the French wherein the major English victory at the 1415 Battle of Agincourt against the numerically odds-on favorite French was due to the newly invented English longbow, used in large numbers by Henry V's archer-heavy, much-smaller army.

The English longbow seems to me a failed illustration, and so to grasp the impact of technology on the morality of warfare, I make arrangements to talk by phone to Major General James Poss, the former U.S. Air Force assistant deputy chief of staff for intelligence, surveillance, and reconnaissance.

Several days in advance of our scheduled call, Major General Poss proves just how astute he is by sending me an online, interactive map whose cranberry-colored dots indicate the locations of dropped bombs, according to the World War II in-full bomb census of London during the Blitz. Zooming in on the map, I count how many buildings on my block were turned into rubble; when I zoom out, the entirety of London is cranberry colored.

After I greet Major General Poss over the phone by thanking him for the map, he volunteers that his English mother was evacuated as a young woman during the London Blitz to East Anglia, where she met and married his father, stationed with the U.S. Air Force.

Having grown up hearing his mother's horrendous stories of London under attack, Major General Poss is not inured to the human consequences of being bombed. He asks that I consider World War II airmen flying at night and dropping bombs on cities and ports without the ability to clearly see what they were bombing. Because it is early in the conversation, I decide not to point out that his suggestion has not assigned an enemy for me to imagine. Instead, he refers only to airmen dropping bombs, no matter their nationality and regardless of whom they were bombing and why. In this way, Major General Poss has given me the impression warfare is primarily about process. He tells me that he is sure that America is better positioned to act morally in twenty-first-century Western warfare, because, he says, "our technology has caught up with our morality."

"The U.S. didn't make a significant aircraft advance in targeting until 1970, during the Vietnam War, with what were called laser-guided weapons," he explains. "But we weren't able to focus on small targets, because you only had a few seconds to strike. Our U-2 reconnaissance aircraft used digital cameras to take snapshots of their targets. We didn't have today's full-action video camera that enables you to loiter, so we could never track a target; it appeared in the moment of a single picture and was gone with the next one. Things changed during the Gulf War with the development of a video-equipped, Predator aircraft, which improved reconnaissance. For example, we were able to discover that each time our planes took off from Saudi Arabia, the Iraqis would pack up their radar equipment and move it under highway bridges with civilian traffic, counting on the fact we would never take out a bridge with civilians on it."

There is a protracted pause. And then the major general does something I did not expect. He refers to Saint Augustine, an early fifth-century Christian theologian and philosopher, and his book *City of God*. Considered a cornerstone of Western thought, the book touches on the undeniable existence of evil and asserts that in defense of oneself and others violence would not be considered immoral.

I ask the major general about the method he used when deciding on a target that would likely risk civilian harm, and he explains that he and his colleagues would pore over every detail of each scenario's estimated casualties and, when necessary, they would "refer up" for final approval.

"If you're talking about conventional air force targets in wartime, there is a very onerous process. We would come up with target nominations—targets that we want to hit—and look at each target; we would consider exactly what we would want to achieve by taking it out. And then we did what is called weapon pairing: we would look at what was required to take that target out with a minimum amount of collateral damage. That's a very sophisticated process, and there is software that assists us in evaluating. The first-stage question is, is the target on a military base with no structures within five hundred feet of it, which means very low collateral damage? And then you go all the way up to what we call Collateral Damage, Level 4, which means you really can't get a weapon in there without causing some damage to what you suspect will be civilian structures. The decision to fire at Level 1 and 2 would be retained by a three-star general. Level 3 and 4 would have to be made by the four-star general at Central Command."

That process involved the web-based construction of a model, which provided a grasp of the specifics: if the bomb is dropped here, it will cause structural damage there, it will cause blast damage there, it will blow out windows in the vicinity of humans, and so on.

What comes first, evaluating the worth of a target after acknowledging that there might be a civilian cost to hitting the target, or identifying the target first, and then weighing the value of that target against the graded 1 through 4 likelihood of civilian injury or death?

"The targets very rarely out-prioritize the collateral damage effects. Despite the established fact that the bridge had radar under it, we would not have taken out the bridge for two reasons. The first reason is that no matter how careful we would have been, there was civilian traffic going over the bridge; the second reason is that destroying the bridge would have damaged the infrastructure of the city, and you don't want to inflict undue suffering to the civilian population to destroy something that has no strategic impact. On the other hand, the real reason we had so many aircraft in Saudi Arabia all of those years had to do with our assignment to take out some twenty bridges on the Euphrates and Tigris Rivers, which would make it impossible for Saddam Hussein to move significant forces into Kuwait after he threatened to do so. In that case, to implement a strategic advantage of preventing him from creating a great deal of collateral damage, we took the risk that by taking out those bridges, we were not doing severe damage to Iraq's infrastructure. As for human life, yes, we took the risk that no one was driving across the bridge at the time."

Major General Poss concludes his argument with a larger point: when atrocities against a great many civilians are likely, preventing their deaths justifies risking the lives of a few. There is a footnote placed at the end of our conversation. According to Major General Poss, after the Vietnam War, fewer American soldiers were willing to believe that the means justify the moral ends.

To understand this means-versus-ends revelation, I turn to Dr. David Rodin for assistance. Dr. Rodin is the co-director of the Oxford Institute for Ethics, Law, and Armed Conflict, a senior fellow at the Carnegie Council for Ethics in International Affairs, and the founder of Principia Advisory, a consulting company that has advised governments, NGOs, and major corporations on ethics.

Whip smart, flop-haired, and incongruently optimistic about humankind despite the field in which he works, Dr. Rodin is a New Zealander who lives in Switzerland but is in London on business. He has accepted my breakfast invitation, and we are stationed in my kitchen when I make the point that war operates comfortably on both ends of the moral scale. I remind him that at one time European rulers—the clever ones, at any rate—took the precaution of requesting the pope's blessing so that they could declare virtuous the atrocities they committed, an example being the vicious Crusades against Islam, which were largely political in purpose. Dr. Rodin concedes this but points to the profound societal alterations that occurred after World War II.

"It took us away from traditional authority figures, governments, corporations, and the church and it empowered us as individuals—now, more than ever before," he tells me. "Technology has played a big role, but there have also been moral shifts, one of them being the enormous rise in the idea of human rights."

—

THE IDEA OF human rights was initially an intellectual conceit, made by theorists, philosophers, and religious communities, before it crystallized into politics and the law. According to Dr. Rodin, it's had a transformative effect in the army as well, and he has been instrumental in repositioning the U.S. Army's moral structure, which, for the very first time, embeds human rights as one of the opening principles.

"It's an acknowledgment that all human beings have certain fundamental rights, the first among which is the right to life," he tells me and then goes on to say that although militaries have duties to aid and rescue others, our most important moral duties, by far, are to not violate the core rights of others.

"Shooting my neighbor in the head is much worse than failing to protect him from an equivalent harm, even if I have contractual or other duties of care toward him," Dr. Rodin says. "This simple fact places a very high burden of justification on the use of force. An enemy can become liable to defensive force if he is responsible for an imminent attack on our rights and if our defensive action is not substantially more harmful than the attack we seek to avert. Otherwise, intentionally killing that person or people is a form of murder."

Dr. Rodin believes that killing is morally justified, but if war is to be permissible, then this is predicated on a just cause, whose pursuit is both proportionate and a last resort.

So when, exactly, do we consider it a last resort, and how, exactly, do we undertake warfare when the sworn enemy is actively seeking to murder innocents in the most gruesome ways?

From the air, according to General Michael Moseley.

General Moseley, former chief of the U.S. Air Force, has spent twenty-two years, off and on, in the Middle East. As a member of the Joint Chiefs of Staff, he also functioned as a military adviser to the secretaries of defense, the National Security Council, and two presidents. As with General Poss, I reach General Moseley by phone. He answers my call in his car, driving through North Carolina. Assuming, as I do, that our conversation is on a speakerphone, I ask General Moseley if he is the only one in the car. He is.

General Moseley is determined to make an important point first. It is not subtle.

"Once a president or prime minister—or whoever it is in a civilian leadership—makes the decision to go to war, in a way, it becomes its own entity. The outcome is never certain, and the conduct along the way is never entirely controlled. It is an environment and a culture unique to itself. I have been in decisional sessions with two presidents, and the discussions were exactly the same: I told them, 'Do not do this . . . do not get us into war unless you are willing to go the whole way, because you are just about to commit sons and daughters and that sacrifice had better be worth it.' There must be an answer to the question, what will it look like when it's done?"

This is General Moseley expressing frustration for what he perceives to be the outcome from the moral dithering of vocal critics. The impression I have of him is that he's not so much unsympathetic as world-weary of war and human nature.

"American governing principles, our philosophical ideas of governance, our values . . . none of these are perfect—we've screwed so many things up along the way—but at the end of the day there is an American notion of fair play and rule of law, which provide a backstop to things," he says. "You've got to remember that war is, in its essence, about killing people and destroying things. Whether it is an enlisted soldier with a rifle who shoots a person or an artillery round that hits something, whether it is from the air, whether it is from the sea, there's no way around the fact it is a hideous act, because you are tasked by your own government to take other people's lives and to destroy property. Despite this, I would say that in the past one hundred years among the Western countries there has been a desire to establish rules in regard to warfare so that, hopefully, we will not use biological and chemical weapons; hopefully, we will never again use nuclear weapons. U.S. officers take courses, sign documents, and take an oath to defend the Constitution; we are legally bound by all government policies that cover the protection of civilians and innocents, adhering to the rules of engagement. Morality is upheld with rules about the treatment of women and of prisoners. There are rules about hospitals and places of worship and of property with cultural and historical importance. That's where General Poss and I spent hundreds of hours with very detailed computer programming and very finite input in the models that helped me mitigate the possibility of collateral damage by the choice of weapons and the timing of a strike or an attack. There is the expectation that in war we will operate within the boundaries of the values that Americans hold dear. Not all countries hold our values, and not everyone believes in war. But if the choice has been made to go to war and to put your military in harm's way, then you accept that there are a number of ways in warfare to deliver ordnance to someone you want killed . . . to deliver deadly force within the rules of engagement."

"And this is increasingly done from the air," I say.

"That's correct. Rough estimates are that over 80 percent of hostiles killed have been from the air since the beginning of the campaign in Afghanistan until where we are now."

"Is the reason for that a political one?" I ask. "Perhaps drones are less an instrument of warfare than a remote and lethal implementer of the U.S. foreign policy."

The general warns me off. He tells me that more often than not the enemies today are groups of violent extremists who cannot be defeated through conventional warfare.

"Don't go down a political road on this one," he tells me. "Remember, a drone is simply the carrier of a weapon."

True. In the literal sense. What generates controversy over the use of drones is its clinical method of frontline combat conducted with anonymity some 7,800 miles away in a climate-controlled command and control center located on the outskirts of Las Vegas, where pilots without planes in front of computer screens launch remote-controlled strikes.

Often operatives track their targets for months, and I cannot help but wonder if they develop a peculiar intimacy with them and their families as they follow them from home to school to mosque.

No matter the method, the point is to kill, says General Moseley.

"A B-2, a Russian MiG-31, a British Typhoon, French Rafale . . . all of these carry a weapon that is dropped from the air through the atmosphere and hits the ground and kills people. Whether it's manned or unmanned doesn't matter. The fact that air strikes have killed more people in Afghanistan has nothing to do with policy and everything to do with the precision of the modern weapons and the accuracy of delivering them from anywhere in the world. It minimizes civilian deaths and exposes the drone operatives to less risk."

I suggest that one can claim that this makes killing too easy. In a tone that leaves no doubt, he rejects that line of thinking.

"It's just as easy to launch a missile from aircraft. The advantage the unmanned system has is that you don't have to employ a lot of people and support equipment. It's a logistical issue, not an operational one and certainly not a policy issue."

General Moseley emphasizes that like pilots providing close air support or dropping bombs, drone operatives do not strike unless there is a thorough assessment of potential cost to innocents. And then he returns to the issue of just how much of a challenge it is—given the West's strict rules of engagement in warfare—that the American military undertakes warfare when the sworn enemy despises those Western values and when that enemy's only rules of engagement are actively to seek to kill innocents.

"The lethal air weapons are the most effective in fighting this kind of enemy. Against other vehicles, against other soldiers, they can see them coming, but with drone strikes, they have no chance, because, quite literally, they can do nothing about it."

"How can it be that in the modern world there can be this kind of war?" I ask.

"Wait a minute," he tells me.

He pulls the car to the side of the road.

"Look, it isn't the first time for that question," he says. "In the late winter, early spring of 1914, no one would have predicted that Europe would be at war at the level they were. No one would have predicted that with the interconnected economies and transportation the enlightened capitals of Berlin, Vienna, Budapest, Paris, Brussels, and Amsterdam . . . that by September we will be killing each other in staggeringly large numbers. Think of the 1920s, when the world has recovered from the nightmare. Think of the intellectuals, the arts, the fashion, and the glittering notions of globalizations . . . but then there is a shift in economies, which was largely responsible for the National Socialists coming to power in Germany. And even then, who would have predicted that within five years we humans would be systematically murdering millions of our fellow humans by gassing them and burning their bodies in ovens?"

There is silence between us.

18

IMMORALITY'S BLACK SUN

> But I own that I cannot see as plainly as others
> do, and as I should wish to do, evidence of
> design and beneficence on all sides of us. There
> seems to me too much misery in the world.

—*Charles Darwin,* The Life and Letters of Charles Darwin

Leo Schenker's blue eyes sparkle just enough mischief to convince anyone that he can still charm the ladies. I know this because his are looking at me in the most delightful way, and this is because I have made the decision to return to New York in order to speak with him. Born and raised in Vienna, now in his eighties, Mr. Schenker is a tall, trim, decidedly handsome man whose tasteful attire suggests that he has a familiar relationship with his tailor.

Leo was one of three brothers. His father was a partner in a company that manufactured scythes crucial to the neighboring countries for them to reap their grain. Leo's carefree childhood was buffered from any real unpleasantness or discomfort until March 12, 1938. That date has its own name, *Anschluss,* and marked the day Austria was annexed to Nazi Germany. That day changed everything in Leo Schenker's life. Leo Schenker is Jewish.

At the time Leo was a boy, Vienna's population of 2 million counted 200,000 Jews. Though Hitler came to power in 1933, Austria's Christian Democratic Party managed to maintain political distance from Nazi Germany for a period of time. That the Austrian newspapers wrote about Hitler and Germany more in connection with politics than in connection with Jews might explain the lack of serious concern felt among most Viennese Jews. But within days of Germany's annexation of Austria, Vienna erupted in anti-Semitic violence. Jewish newspapers were shut, Jewish actors, musicians, and journalists were arrested, Jewish stores were ransacked, and Jewish women— some directed to wear their best clothes—were forced to scrub the streets with toothbrushes. People were beaten; others were taken to Gestapo headquarters and never returned.

Soon after Nazi troops arrived in the city, Adolf Eichmann established the Central Office for Jewish Emigration. In exchange for their citizenship and property rights, Jews— applying for passports to gain entry to countries likely to turn them back at the borders—were issued visas with a fourteen-day expiration date.

Leo's parents tarried dangerously, waiting until Leo and his two brothers were out of school in June before leaving their homeland. Leo's father had a scythe factory in a Polish town, not far from the German border, where the family resumed their lives. As the Nazis escalated their policies of degradation against the Jews, the Schenkers felt increasingly vulnerable living as close as they were to the German border. They moved again, this time to Kraków.

On September 1, 1939, Germany invaded Poland. Three days later, trying to outrun the murderous upheaval yet again, the Schenkers loaded their possessions in a car and drove east. Having run out of gas—with no fuel available to be bought— they purchased a horse and cart and continued their journey until they reached the Polish Ukraine, a territory occupied at the time by the Soviet Union, which had invaded Poland from the east without a formal declaration of war. In Lwów (now

Lviv, Ukraine), the Schenkers shared an apartment with a Russian officer and his wife. Leo's father, who spoke Romanian, found a job with the Romanian delegation.

The only source of accurate information on events outside Lwów came from BBC Radio's reporting the news each night in German. In June 1941, Russia entered the war against Germany, and that same month Lwów fell to the German army. Within an hour of the Nazis' arrival in the city, Ukrainian nationalists joined forces and went on a deadly rampage. During three consecutive days, two thousand Jews were dragged out of their homes, beaten, and killed. The Nazis brought a halt to the killings when they began to implement their own agenda. They cordoned off the northern portion of the city and designated it a Jewish ghetto.

Rather than risking the unpredictability of the Gestapo outside the ghetto, the Schenkers decided that they would be safer living within its crowded confines. Making it to the ghetto's front gate was a gamble; German police shot thousands of elderly and sick trying to get there by crossing the rail bridge, which became known as the Bridge of Death.

The Schenkers managed to cross the ghetto's threshold, though once they arrived, the little they were able to bring with them was confiscated by SS officers. They moved into a single room shared with another family.

In September 1941, the Germans converted a mill machinery factory in a suburb of Lwów into a labor camp where those from the ghetto fit enough were sent, including Leo and his older brother, Kurt. Named after the street on which it was located, Janowska, it became a portal to a hideous other dimension. Built next to it was a concentration camp to house the skeletal prisoners forced to labor in carpentry and ironwork.

So out of the scale of human experience was Janowska that no one could imagine the depths of the depravity and sadism thriving there. Atrocities became an unremarkable part of the daily routine. People were starved and tortured. Some were shot in front of others. In the hierarchy of fear among prisoners, the line between compassion and inhumanity wavered and then vanished. Everyone did whatever was needed to stay alive.

"If someone told you to lick his boots, you would do it if it meant it would prevent you from being tortured" was how Mr. Schenker put it. "With hunger, with beatings, with torture, you can make a person behave like a dog," he said. "Prisoners stole food from each other. They informed on each other. The survival instinct is much stronger than one knows or realizes."

I asked him if he was religious.

"From what I've seen during my life, religious people suffered more," Mr. Schenker said. "There were many people who lost their lives because of religion, but that is not the purpose of living."

"Do you think that being religious under the circumstances you've described increased the likelihood that one was willing to act morally and in ways that might jeopardize his own safety on someone else's behalf?"

"It wasn't about morality. It was about survival. Whether you were religious or nonreligious, very few were willing to help others if it meant risking yourself."

We discuss the relationship between morality and freedom, and whether moral judgments can be made at all when one has no control over one's life, when the reality of one's life defies comparison. In order to survive, Mr. Schenker became adept at making instant judgments, not only about the guards and those who tortured, but also about the fellow inmates equally intent on surviving. Whether or not that entailed becoming an agent himself of the cruelty that had surrounded him, only Mr. Schenker can say, but I've no doubt it required him to become good at being less moral for that period of time and under those circumstances.

Janowska became a transit camp with its own selection process: those classified fit to work remained there to be subjected to unspeakable suffering; the majority, rejected as unfit, were either deported to the Belzec extermination camp or shot at the

Piaski ravine close by. Fate intervened, and Leo and his brother were sent to a work farm not far away whose purpose was to grow fruits and vegetables for the Gestapo. Thirty-five people worked the land supervised by a single SS officer with the sole power to kill any or all of them. But unlike at Janowska, there was enough food grown on the farm so that no one starved to death.

Each week, the brothers took a truck to deliver produce to the Gestapo headquarters, where they saw and heard prisoners being tortured. Every fourth week, Leo and his brother were given a day leave to the ghetto. They always returned to the camp; had they not, the other workers would have been shot. During one of their leaves, Leo's father managed to slip poison pills to his sons and told them that if the time came when there was no more hope, now they had an option.

In March 1942, anyone still living in the ghetto was deported to Belzec and became ash. When, in August, Leo's parents were taken from their home, the Nazis neglected to look behind the open door where Leo's mother had hidden her youngest son, Henry. Leo's parents were loaded on a railcar; they were killed shortly after arriving at Belzec.

Leo Schenker will never understand why the SS officer in charge of the work farm told Leo in advance that the farm would be liquidated. Forewarned in the morning that everyone in the camp would be shot in the afternoon, Leo and his brother delivered produce to the Gestapo headquarters and went missing after unloading the truck.

Despite escaping death that day, both believed it was the end. They had no money. There was no place to go. By now, there were no Jews left living in Lwów. Their parents had been killed. It was assumed that their brother, too, was dead. They were alive, but their world was gone. With no money, convinced they would be discovered by the Nazis and killed—or, worse, tortured—Leo and Kurt, finally the agents of their own destiny, agreed to a double suicide.

What saved them from impossible circumstances was the improbable.

THE POISON MADE them sick, but not so much so that they were unable to crawl their way to safety and hide for the time it took them to obtain forged identity papers documenting them as German Poles. Like their parents, Leo and his brother were put on a train from Lwów. Instead of transporting them to their deaths, it brought them both to safety; for it was at that point in the war when auxiliary forces were being recruited from conquered nationals in German-occupied territories. An arbitrary whim of nature had given the brothers the same Aryan features as their persecutors. They were also fluent in German and Polish, to which Leo and his brother owed their lives. No one so much as asked to see their forged identity papers before they boarded the train to the Black Sea port of Sevastopol.

Kurt was assigned to one unit and given duties at the radio station; Leo, assigned to another, became the office manager in a car repair shop. They were paid for their work. Hiding in plain sight, they went to the movies and ate in restaurants. When they were asked to join colleagues for a drink, never did they bring up the subject of Jews, nor did they ever hear talk of them. Leo and his brother embodied an alternative reality and another kind of truth.

"As an undetected Jew among Nazis—the very people responsible for systematically murdering your people, including your parents—did you feel it was a betrayal to your faith or its moral code?" I ask.

"Once again, it had nothing to do with morals. It had to do with survival."

"And so you put aside your moral being in order to survive?"

"Yes."

"How and when did you manage to retrieve that part of yourself?"

"With time" is the answer.

When Russian troops advanced on Sevastopol, Leo and his brother were evacuated to the Romanian border, but to different locations. Leo's unit went to Odessa, where he found a way of deserting the German army and escaping to Bucharest. There, Leo heard that there were three steamers taking Jews to Israel.

It was much easier for him to become a member of the German army than it was for him to become a Jew again. He was denied passage to Israel until a family friend living in Bucharest vouched that he was a Jew. At the time Leo arrived in Israel, he was not yet twenty. Three years on, he was able to afford to move to New York, where he married and became a successful businessman. Leo Schenker had learned what was required to endure the unendurable by finding something within himself that the darkness couldn't take away.

Leo's older brother, Kurt, suffered a breakdown during his evacuation from Sevastopol, and I cannot help but wonder if this was the result of being separated from Leo for the first time in the years they struggled to stay alive. Kurt was shot by the Nazis, not as a Jew, but as a mentally ill German. Leo's younger brother, Henry, as a boy hidden behind an open door, made it to safety. He lives in Houston.

Leo Schenker survived a life of death during a God-abandoned suspension between the two. He spoke of it with eerie self-containment, making no mention of the moral issues that had confronted him, and not for a moment did he express his feelings. "No one would understand or is able to imagine," he tells me. "There's no point."

No one would argue the enormity of what happened in the Holocaust. It defied reason. It changed mankind's conception of itself. It forced most to question the existence of God. But I believe there is a point, and it is this: in fact, somebody—many somebodies—did imagine its cruelty and horror, and then they made it happen.

The carnage that followed Mr. Schenker during his adolescence and into his young adulthood is too great to comprehend. The majority of Jews—some 65,000—who stayed behind in Vienna were deported to concentration camps. Of that number, only 2,000 survived. It was determined that over 200,000 people were murdered in Janowska. There were no Jews left in Lwów by the time Leo's parents were sent to Belzec, where between 430,000 and 500,000 Jews are believed to have been murdered.

Progressive eighteenth- and nineteenth-century philosophers pondered if, by behaving better day by day, we, as a species, gradually become better and more moral. The twentieth century answers no. The Holocaust is not the only evidence. China's Cultural Revolution saw thirty million people die in a period of ten years; Pol Pot, the Cambodian revolutionary, led the Khmer Rouge, and his murderous policies when he presided over a total dictatorship caused the deaths of 21 percent of what was then Cambodia's population. In a time closer to our own, we have watched deliberate famines and ethnic cleansing in Africa and Bosnia and, now, the Middle East. Images stream across our computer screens to remind us that mankind's barbarity lurks just below the surface of civilization and that in the blink of an eye it can be tapped to obliterate anything resembling morality.

PART FIVE

*The Future, or
Something Like It*

19

THE MORAL VAGARIES OF MAKING BABIES

Sometimes I've believed as many as six
impossible things before breakfast.

—*the Queen in* Through the Looking-Glass

Some twenty years ago, I was having breakfast in L.A. with a friend, Laura, when I heard what I could not have imagined. We'd finished our meal and were ordering coffee when Laura spotted someone she recognized on the other side of the restaurant. The woman joined us, and she and Laura began to discuss two other women they both knew but I didn't. My mind wandered before being yanked back by the unexpectedly conjoined words "sperm reprobate."

Sperm generally comes into play privately or within the context of biology in, say, a doctor's office or a scientific journal, not in a social setting and certainly not where food is being served. At least that's what I was taught. It is true that L.A. is an encyclopedia of everything weird, and at the time my husband and I—along with our infant son—had only recently moved there from New York. *Perhaps it was a colloquialism,* I thought to myself. Even so, it seemed a peculiar thing to say, and I decided to confirm that what I heard was what Laura actually meant.

"My husband was disinvited to Susan's birthday party," she

repeated for my benefit. "And when asked why, they told him it was because he was a sperm reprobate."

I had known Peter for the same ten years I had Laura. None of my imaginings could point him out as a reprobate. He was a talented architect with a steady disposition and a kind heart. Just as confounding to me was why the extremely personal aspect of Peter's manhood was being slandered and, on a lesser note, how it became responsible for disinviting him to a birthday party.

"I still don't understand," I told Laura. "What has Peter done?"

Peter, it turned out, had done quite a lot.

Laura is a journalist whose habit it is to make things clear, and so she explained the situation matter-of-factly. Susan was indeed one of the two women under discussion. She was also one-half of a lesbian couple determined to parent a child. The agreement between her and her partner was simple: the two of them would attempt to get pregnant, with one discontinuing her efforts as soon as the other was successfully impregnated. Peter agreed to be the sperm donor for both women.

Avoiding a rush to judgment, I asked Laura for a fuller understanding of the slanderous aspect of her story: Specifically, what was it that made Peter a sperm reprobate?

According to Laura, it had to do with the decision by the two women to forgo freezing Peter's semen. When, at a later time, I had a chance to contemplate the story's more nuanced aspects, I couldn't help but wonder if the fact that the women were singled out as extremely attractive might have had something to do with Peter's enthusiasm to deliver his commitment in person. Be that as it may, all parties were in agreement on the process.

Conflicts arose, though not the kind I might have foretold. The two women didn't live close to Peter and Laura, and the commute took Peter hours in snarled L.A. traffic. There was another complication to do with timing. Because the women had different monthly cycles, they ovulated at different stages of the month. It turned out that Peter was expected to be available more often than was planned. The women were on a regime of estrogen to improve their chances of conceiving. Suffering from severe mood swings, they became what Laura described as "high maintenance."

Peter was overcome by exhaustion as he tried in vain to keep pace with the hormonally charged women. When their unsparing demands caused him to miss an important business meeting, he decided to bow out of his sperm duties. Having reneged on his agreement, Peter was no longer welcomed at Susan's upcoming birthday party. All things being equal, it was her partner who accused him of being a sperm reprobate.

Unbelievably funny and embarrassingly not funny at the same time, Peter's story featured so much unexpected information in such a short period of time that it induced in me a type of mental double vision, and I was left with nothing to say.

That was not the case by the time I returned home.

"Just how attractive are the lesbians?" was my husband's first question after being debriefed.

Even though my husband's male perspective revealed what I thought to be a less-than-laudable sensibility, both of us were equally confused about what to feel. Laura and Peter were principled individuals, deeply committed to their marriage. They had been in full command of what was a mutual decision, which prevented Peter's behavior from being considered adulterous. Yes, Laura and Peter had proven a more unconventional couple than I thought, and, admittedly, it rattled the abacus of my perception of marriage. But unconventionality does not necessarily make for unethical behavior or—for that matter— even bad behavior.

Though I wasn't entirely sure about my husband's concluding argument that Peter was an inadvertent protagonist in a modern-day morality tale, I decided that the issue was not one of unethical practices as much as it was a forward-leaning attitude I didn't share.

If you thought there was an end to this matter, and that

this situation would throw up no further ethical conundrums, you would be wrong. As is often the case with human behavior, just when you assume it can't get any stranger, it does.

IT HAD BEEN six months since I left my position as a book publisher in New York to launch a magazine in L.A. Sandra, one of the magazine's columnists, was getting married. I volunteered to organize a small celebration in my home and suggested she invite a few of her friends.

Sandra's friends appeared to me as edgy variations on an alternative lifestyle. I nonetheless took a traditional approach and acknowledged the happy occasion by offering a toast to the bride-to-be. Suggesting Sandra would be facing marital questions I had not when I married, I jested that one such modern-day decision would be if she allowed her husband's sperm out of the house. It was meant to be a glib comment. Unfortunately, Julia, Sandra's militant friend, did not see it that way.

During the time it took for cake to be served, Julia told of her brother and sister, both gay, both in long-term relationships, both wanting children. Her brother inseminated her sister's partner with the understanding that the baby be given to him if his partner impregnated his sister, who would keep that baby for her own. It might have been easier if Julia had drawn a Venn diagram for me.

After the guests left, I walked Sandra to her parked car.

"I hope you enjoyed the send-off," I told her, ignoring my own discomfort with what had occurred during the course of it.

"Julia was out of line," said Sandra. "And what's going on with her hair?" she asked earnestly. "What's that about?"

By the time I came back inside, a fog of moral confusion had settled around me. To donate sperm, as was the case with Peter, is one thing; to manufacture a baby knowing it would be swapped for another is another thing entirely, and it bothered me. Still, I believed Julia when she insisted that regardless of the method by which they were conceived, the babies would be loved unquestionably.

Twenty years on, the same two babies are young adults. They hail from a generation unfamiliar with the origins of the derogatory word "bastard" and who don't believe in any single way of creating a family.

MAPPING A POST-GAY CULTURE

Gay or straight? So what?

—*Willie Nelson*

At this point in my undertaking to understand which way the moral wind is blowing, it seems fairly clear to me that, in the West, change is less likely to come from the direction of institutional authority and more from the broad consideration of current events and social power. The church's unwillingness to recognize this has forced the role of religion into a series of retreats. This appears especially true for issues pertaining to sex.

When religion proclaims that one way of having sex is moral while another is not, two things are bound to happen: either that kind of sex will continue to be enjoyed out of sight, or it will become a battlefield in the open. For centuries, virtually all religions have denounced homosexuality—Catholicism in particular—and so it is now supremely ironic that predominantly Catholic Ireland has become the first country to legalize gay marriage.

AMONG THE KEY figures responsible for this counterintuitive outcome are a civil rights activist—claiming that the standing law infringed on his right to privacy—who took the attorney general to the High Court over the criminalization of homosexual acts; a feminist theologian who was a former CEO of the National Women's Council of Ireland; the minister of justice and equality, who was previously appointed as the minister for children and youth affairs; Ireland's first openly gay minister; a former president of Ireland who was from a devout Catholic family and had a gay son; one of Ireland's most famous openly gay sportsmen; an Irish novelist, critic, and poet, cited as one of Britain's top three hundred intellectuals by the *Observer;* and a well-known current affairs blogger with an impressively large social media following. Each one of these people imagined the same different moral alternative.

"Did cultural osmosis change the law, or was it that the law had no choice but to pivot?" is the double-barreled question that begins my phone conversation with Robert Hofler, the author of several books exploring heterosexual and nonheterosexual themes.

"I can't speak for what transpired in Ireland" is his careful qualifier. "But in America, it was the courts that forced people to acknowledge a change, though, by the time the law changed, the taboo of being gay had already lost hold."

Sexplosion, one of Mr. Hofler's books, focused its narrative attention on the four years, between 1968 and 1972, during which there was a surprising number of movies, novels, plays, and even TV shows trespassing on what had been conventional sexual boundaries.

Mr. Hofler names a few examples: *Myra Breckinridge, Portnoy's Complaint, Couples, Hair, Oh! Calcutta!, The Boys in the Band, Midnight Cowboy, Last Tango in Paris.*

"What struck me was how much gay subject matter also came into play during that same period," says Mr. Hofler, who is gay and was raised Roman Catholic before deciding he was more comfortable as an atheist. "In the 1970s, gay men took being outcasts and made it into something glamorous."

I tell him that when I arrived in New York just out of college in the late 1970s, the city was awash in sex—both straight and gay—but my sense was that there was an inordinate amount of gay sex.

"Yes, well, if one believed the reports during that decade, a gay man was more likely to have a venereal disease than a female prostitute, the inference being that he was having more sexual encounters," says Mr. Hofler.

Why was that? I ask.

"I think it had to do with the fact that gays had just emerged from an environment of oppression to find themselves at the advent of tremendous liberation and having sex was part of that."

"But why so much of it?"

"It's complicated," Mr. Hofler tells me. "Had you been gay, you would have also been in conflict: in conflict not only with society, but also in conflict with yourself because you were most likely disenfranchised from your own family."

"Are you suggesting that self-loathing manifests itself in the relentless pursuit of the kind of sex that others considered perverse?"

"Possibly. But don't underestimate the simple fact that gay men are men."

Mr. Hofler's "men are men" comment shares ground with my belief that there is a fundamental difference between the sexes when it comes to the pursuit of sex.

"One thing that continues to amaze me—and I think it has to do with testosterone—is that we're in an age when there are a number of major female politicians," he says. "The U.S. Senate is now up to twenty and Congress, I believe, has an even greater percentage of females. Where are the female sex scandals? And yet we continue to have all these political sex scandals involving men. I think that says something about testosterone."

In my mind, I begin to count the number of women assuming political power on the global stage: Hillary Clinton in America; the German chancellor, Angela Merkel; the IMF's managing director, Christine Lagarde; the chair of the Federal Reserve, Janet Yellen; the leader of the Scottish National Party, Nicola Sturgeon; the mayor of Rome, Virginia Raggi. They all possess unalloyed pragmatism and—with the exception at times of Hillary Clinton, with her documented history of unsavory dealings—a deep-seated common sense. Though they are similar ages to their male counterparts, I can't imagine any one of these women caught out in a sex scandal.

"Women are more risk averse than men; it could be that they're wired that way, or maybe it's that they have no choice because the double standard is still hanging over them," I tell Mr. Hofler. "My point is that a man caught with his pants down is considered foolish, but a woman responsible for the same kind of sexual escapade would fall from grace, and it would shatter her reputation."

"Good point," concedes Mr. Hofler. "But, as I've said, it could be that, simply put, the majority of men—straight or gay—are driven by sex more than women."

Mr. Hofler's less-is-more proposition intrigues me.

"So, if you were to consider gender, rather than sexuality, do you think that given the opportunity, heterosexual men would be just as promiscuous as gay men?"

"Probably not," says Mr. Hofler.

"Why not?"

"There are dynamics at play."

"Like what?"

"To begin with, logistics. To serve a gay man in a bar was illegal not so long ago."

Mr. Hofler explains that the end of Prohibition was brought about with an agreement among the people who mattered that whatever appeared immoral that congregated around the serving of liquor in bars would have to go—including gays.

"There was no choice for gay men but to seek out sex in restrooms and parks. What that did was to create a world of secret, forbidden sex. Gays fetishized the hypersexual aspects so that even after the bars stopped being raided, they continued to go to the truck stops and the West Side piers for sex. That was when the decor of the gay bars changed from perfectly respectable looking to ones with dark, rough-hewn interiors. There was a great deal of sex, and no one was using condoms because, unlike heterosexual sex, one need not be concerned with issues of birth control. It got to the point that men were taking penicillin before weekends on Fire Island, where sex was had in multiples."

MR. HOFLER'S LONG-TERM partner died of AIDS.

"My generation came out at the same time that the health crisis occurred. There's now an entire generation that didn't live through the horror, and I've heard about a lot of guys going on Grindr [a gay hookup site], where they negotiate the kind of sex they're willing to have in advance of having it, and then they all take PrEP [a drug taken to protect from AIDS] and feel they don't have to use condoms."

He pauses and then adds, "It's given me a negative view of today's gay morality."

I move the discussion onto the topic of same-sex marriage, and Mr. Hofler identifies a paradigm shift in conventional marriage that made the other possible.

"When straight marriage was no longer for life and it didn't have to include having children, the old excuses of denying marriage to a same-sex couple were no longer applicable. In 2002 and 2003, the two state courts dragged their constituencies kicking and screaming to accept change. That was followed by defeats in some thirty other state courts, all covered by the media. The American media seems to thrive on polarizing topics; it played on the topic of legalizing same-sex marriage because it raised ratings. On the other end of the argument was the Republican Party, and they played on it because a few of their candidates won elections by including constitutional amendments on the ballot dictating marriage had to be between a man and a woman only. With all the media exposure, what became obvious was that objecting to same-sex marriage had far less to do with religion than it had to do with personal prejudice."

It is futile to argue the point that the issue of sex becomes its most emphatic when it has something to resist. It was only when pushing against the status quo, the courts, and conservative politicians, that sexual choice had its way.

There is an abundance of sexual identities that underpin the changing patterns of contemporary life. Rather than considering themselves completely gay or straight, the number of people describing themselves as bisexual in the U.K. has jumped by 45 percent in three years according to official statistics, suggesting that more young people in particular have a fluid view of sexuality.

It happens that a week after my phone discussion with Mr. Hofler, London has installed traffic lights with diversity symbols (including one that features the symbol for transgender people) on the green lights to tell pedestrians that it's safe to cross the roads around Trafalgar Square. Under the shadow of Nelson's column, no less, bisexuality has moved into the mainstream of British life.

I write to Mr. Hofler that the velocity of change with which the West has legally and societally adapted to accommodate the range of gender identities still surprises me. He writes back that, with so much sexual choice, we've entered a curiously murky area. "Heretofore, homosexuals have said that sexual orientation is not a choice: you're born that way. But isn't being asked to choose your own gender the same thing as saying it's a choice?"

His is an unanswered question, but the irreversible fact is that societal recognition of sexual diversity has produced radical shifts in personal and public lives. It has transformed the family unit, and it has called on new and different methods of making babies.

I'm not sure if the domestication of same-sex partners will follow the lead of what is considered the fundamentally heterosexual value system, but I do know that those who look back on what they believe was an age of social capital and family stability are those who no longer matter.

21

IS IT PROGRESS IF WE BARTER WITH ETHICS?

*If you don't know where you are going,
you'll end up someplace else.*

—*Yogi Berra*

For millions of years, humans have had sex in order to produce new generations. Today, human reproduction is defined in more semantic than substantial terms, and there are a number of ways to produce babies, each with its own price tag.

The cost in the United States for egg donations varies from $4,000 to $8,000; for attractive donors, such as actresses, models, and high-scoring Ivy League students, it runs into tens of thousands of dollars. Surrogacy in America, including agency fees and insurance, can exceed $200,000.

U.K. laws prevent an individual from paying a woman to have one's baby or drawing up a binding contract, so British parents pay for foreign surrogates, and, primarily because of the pricing, they are looking increasingly to eastern European countries such as Ukraine and Georgia, where women charge as little as $18,000 to carry and deliver a child, compared with $30,000 for the same in India.

Due to what has been China's one-child policy implemented to control the country's overpopulation—due, also, to the overwhelming pressure for couples to produce boys—it is not unheard of, still, for parents in China to abort female fetuses. Prenatal sonograms, which identify their children's gender, are against the law. But the rich purchase their own sonogram machines, and decisions to terminate pregnancies based on the sex do not necessarily include ethical considerations, not in the Western sense of morals. Nor, by the way, do the government's recently loosened policies toward one-child families (in light of the rapidly aging population) and its progressively more relaxed attitude toward female babies (due to the increasing surplus of young Chinese men without brides). These two very serious changes in China have nothing to do with morality but are, instead, unambiguously on the side of reason.

If we in the West think of ourselves as ethically more advanced than China regarding gender selection, we need to be reminded that our own values are at the behest not of morality but of varying Western laws. For example, the practice of in vitro gender selection is allowed only for medical reasons in many European countries and the U.K., while in America a pioneer of in vitro gender selection, Dr. Daniel Potter, has made a tidy fortune trademarking a particularly effective process for gender selection. "Experts in achieving family balancing," explains the home page of Potter's clinic's website, and European and U.K. couples who can afford it come to the United States so that they can legally designate the sex of their baby.

Married couples in China must register with local family-planning authorities before they have a baby. Women having a baby out of wedlock often face fines. Egg freezing is illegal unless you can present a marriage certificate and identity cards for both husband and wife, along with a pregnancy permit. I cannot think where and how one acquires the last of these stamped documents, but I can tell you that, if asked, the majority of young women in China today would most likely support the right of single women to freeze their eggs. And, like those in the U.K. who can afford to circumvent U.K. law that prevents them from selecting the gender of their baby by flying to America with their checkbooks, so too do Chinese women who, barred by law from freezing their eggs, fly to America for that procedure if and when they can afford to. The L.A.-based company Southern California Reproductive Center sells trips to undergo the process legally. Not including travel expenses, the cost for the procedure is $10,000, along with an $800 annual storage fee.

THE FOOD AND Drug Administration is currently evaluating medical procedures that, if successful, will provide genetically modified beings. But the FDA, a regulatory organization whose responsibilities cover only the scientific aspects of a drug, insists that any ethical issues are outside its scope.

New techniques now enable DNA to be altered and edited. Is this moral progress or technological advancement, or are they one and the same? Looking not that far ahead to opportunities to enhance a more desirable physical and neural state, fertility pioneers have spoken out against the moral climate created by wealthy childless couples with access to scientific developments in the booming in vitro fertilization industry. In another fifty years, do we really think that we will leave the conception of our children, or their intelligence, or the color of their eyes to chance? Some biologists are of the belief that there should be an indefinite ban on inheritable alternatives to the human genome; others do not. And with no jurisdiction over gene-editing projects, the morality of genetic tinkering is open-ended.

It is an ideologically tangled age. Those who can afford it draw their own moral lines, while medical advancements that might have taken a century of trial and error to evolve occur in a matter of years, and what seems improbable will eventually become the norm.

More than thirty years ago, the Canadian author Margaret Atwood wrote of such things in her 1985 dystopian novel, *The*

Handmaid's Tale. At the time, it was described as speculative fiction. The novel is set in a quasi-Christian theocracy, which has overthrown the U.S. government after a terrorist attack (blamed on Islamic extremists), and the new regime quickly consolidates its power by reorganizing society based on an Old Testament–inspired social and religious ultraconservatism. Individuals are segregated by categories: sex, occupation, and caste. The new government accesses financial records, labeled by gender and stored electronically, and takes away women's rights. The most fertile women are assigned to reproduce for barren wives of the elite.

It is a bit daunting to acquaint myself with Ms. Atwood's fifty-year body of work in anticipation of meeting her, to which she has kindly agreed. She writes poetry, short stories, children's books, criticism, and radio scripts—all consistently and brilliantly well.

I've flown back to New York in order to speak to her the day before she is launched onto a national book tour for her recent novel. Ours is a morning meeting in the hotel in which she is staying. I recognize her from across the lobby; she greets me with a firm handshake and a convivial smile.

After seating ourselves at a quiet table in the corner of the hotel café, we realize that the venue is self-service, and I volunteer to get the coffee. There's a queue in front of the counter, and every version of coffee is being customized. Fearful that my wait will waste the time she's given me, I return to Ms. Atwood empty-handed and suggest that I revisit the coffee line once it's thinned out.

In her prose and poetry, Ms. Atwood expresses herself in exact terms. So too in conversation. If her manner were not so charming and her voice so gentle, she might come across as intimidating.

"When considering morality, you need to begin with the fact that we come with certain building blocks," she tells me. "Anyone who has raised a child knows that a three-year-old's first need is for information, as in 'What is this?' Then comes,

'Is it good or is it bad?' The judiciary enters a bit later with 'It's not fair.' So what does this mean . . . that children do that?"

I think I know the answer, but I am feeling pressured to make a good first impression, and so I am relieved that Ms. Atwood answers her own question.

"All social animals recognize other social animals of their kind as individuals, and they all have ways of interacting with each other because it's detrimental to be in conflict. Wolves do it. Chimpanzees do it. Elephants do it. As do we. That's the point. We have more variations, but there are still fundamental understandings, because we have been given the basic Lego set."

"So you think the basic Lego set is already in place, no matter where or under which circumstances we are born?" I ask.

"Epigenetics would claim so."

This is the time for me to try the coffee line again. While waiting at the counter, I look up the definition of "epigenetics" on my iPhone. It's the theory that "the embryo develops progressively by stages, influenced by its internal and external environment, forming structures that were not originally present in the egg."

By the time I return to the table with our coffee, Ms. Atwood has thought of other things I should know about morality.

"In the very broad sweep of things, how people get the food they're going to eat—how they make a living—changes the moral direction according to what that method is," she explains. "Among the hunter-gatherers, there was more interpersonal violence. Why? They were nomads. There was no one place, and so they didn't have a prison system. If someone is threatening your group, you kill them, or they would kill you. Farming creates a food surplus, enabling social hierarchy . . . kings and priests and food to support an army . . . all of this came with farming. With fossil fuel and cheap energy, you don't need upper-body strength anymore . . . just with a keyboard, you can become a powerful person. Thus the entry of women into the white-collar workforce."

We discuss the relationship between the source of food and energy and that of a society's moral values and that those values set in place—for a time—what is right, what is wrong, what we approve of, what we disapprove of. The slavery issue in the South, for example, was driven largely by the economy.

"When you're talking about morality—what people think is right and wrong—you have to peel back the issue by asking yourself, 'Why did they approve or disapprove of these things? How were or are they making a living?'"

Given what I've heard in my interviews with those in business, law, and politics, it seems to me that money has a great deal to do with modern morality.

"No, not entirely, but, yes, you can't ignore it."

The caffeine has kicked, and now I am racing ahead with what I know about the selfish gene. A grin breaks on her lips. She listens patiently while I express bitter disappointment that Swedes have debunked the "women and children first" assumption when it came to disasters. Seeing the obvious distress this has caused me, Ms. Atwood is kind enough to put things in perspective with the straightforward assessment that we are all born with a greater or lesser capacity for virtue and enlightenment.

"I believed that at one time," I tell her.

"We have both a selfish gene and an altruistic gene," she insists.

"I fear that the selfish gene is stronger," I tell her.

"The altruistic gene is also very strong," she says, and then she reassures me that counterbalancing the undertow pulling us toward the selfish gene is a sense of goodness that directs us to an eminently moral place.

My thoughts swim along a darker current. "With all due respect, that's the optimism in you. I had it before I began interviewing people."

"It's not optimism," she replies. "It's biology."

If Ms. Atwood is correct, that biology is the bedrock of morality, I wonder what that means for the robots.

22

PROGRAMMING MORALITY IN ROBOTS
(THEY'LL SHOW US HOW)

> Like the chorus of Greek drama they will speak
> As many, but in the first person singular.
>
> —*from "The Robots," a poem by Robert Pinsky*

The stream of migrant workers in China from small towns and villages seeking employment in Chinese factories has been reduced to a trickle in a relatively short period of time. This reduction of the workforce, along with an unprecedented growth of its aging population, is shrinking China's labor pool, which is increasing the cost for its manufacturers, which is decreasing their exports, which is slowing their gross domestic product, which is why they are developing robotic factory workers.

Other countries are also building robots: for the workplace in general, and for factories in particular. It has been forecast that over the next thirty years, robotic employment and automation in clerical and logistical occupations will put at risk some 47 percent of America's jobs and 35 percent of jobs in the U.K. New jobs to replace the old are emerging at a painstakingly slow pace. In short, over a third of all existing jobs in both the United States and the U.K. could be made obsolete by technology and automation. Meanwhile, Google, Facebook, Amazon, and Baidu have joined the arms race for artificial intelligence to assist the disabled, look after the elderly, handle domestic chores, and even carry out routine, low-invasive surgery. For these duties and more, we will improve the robots' communication skills by giving them the power of speech.

All well and good. But there are robots and there are robots.

Scientists at the Interdisciplinary Center in Herzliya, Israel, are developing "safe haven" robots, which they hope will encourage people to share their troubles so as to be helped to feel more confident and attractive. A Taiwanese company has created a toddler-size robot that can move around a home on its own and join the family, not unlike a pet. The Japanese, too, are developing androids more humanlike than machine. At MIT, efforts are being made to design computers to recognize human emotions. South Korea is keen for robots outfitted with weapons to protect its border.

How is any of this possible? you ask.

All of us made it so. We—the ever-increasing, always-connected Internet users—are generating a plethora of data—sometimes willingly, sometimes without knowing it—from our ubiquitous computers, tablets, and cell phones. To put it in plain English: when processed into recognized patterns, that data enables algorithms to develop an increasingly precise awareness of context. Both the question and the concern are whether self-improving computers will eventually rival the human brain.

As someone determined to feel as much as I can, I admit that I am sometimes an unworthy steward of logic. The way I think is part of who I am, and depersonalizing the brain has no appeal whatsoever to me. Neither am I convinced that science always has the answers, so it doesn't bother me that the complexities of the brain deny psychiatry the clear biological markers it is looking for. I say, keep the head doctors guessing.

I grant you: we humans spend a great deal of our lives in dead thought. Our minds move within the limits of our faulty characters. We often miss the facts in front of our eyes. We are easily lulled by lethargy, which invites us to retreat into numbing indifference. Even when we intend to accomplish things, our brain can lead us into an almost surreal state of incompetence. And so I am willing to imagine an improved efficiency if ours was a brain that didn't suffer from hormonal spikes, banal sentimentality, emotional turbulence, and calcified prejudice. Absent the messy influences of love, jealousy, and fear, there would be less possibility of overreacting and doing something stupid.

OUR FACTUAL PRECISION, too, would benefit from a robot brain. Left to its own devices, the human brain is a notoriously gifted inventor of the truth, or whatever seems to be true at the moment. Rather than creating a feedback loop of inaccuracies, a robot brain would be indebted solely to its programmatic cognition.

Hierarchical pattern recognition might be a soulless way of thinking, but the case for that proposition is appealingly straightforward for those who insist that if we were to eliminate fault-prone psychology and irrational behavior that reside in our brain, it would yield far more efficient thinking. On the other hand, not everything civilization has to offer is the product of intelligence. It is the insatiable curiosity we humans have and unbridled imagination that move us forward.

While we debate the obvious value and the possible threat of artificial intelligence, technology is sprinting past our opinions on either side of the argument with an inevitability of more and more sophisticated robots.

Today, robots are guided by an understanding of their physical selves and are capable of adapting to injuries by adjusting themselves in real time, just as a child learns a skill. Theirs is more of an operational morality in the hands of their operators. These robots are unlikely to enslave the human race, but advances are swiftly moving to the point where the most sophisticated devices will no longer simply be tools but be agents in their own right. We'd better start thinking about whether we want that or not, because, even though artificial intelligence doesn't deserve its title yet, speculation has it that by 2022 robots will have the capacity to evaluate the ethical ramifications of their actions, and according to the projections based on their increasing sophistication, robot brains based on computers will begin to rival human intelligence by 2050.

Determined to take matters into their own, collective and human hands, members of the European Parliament want to declare autonomous robots "electronic persons" to which are assigned legally enforced areas of accountability and with the human owners' assuming responsibility not unlike that of a parent company owning a subsidiary. The owners would be expected to pay premiums into a state fund to cover the cost of any harm.

Making us aware of the importance of a liberal arts education, the members put things in literary perspective. "From Mary Shelley's Frankenstein's monster to the classical myth of Pygmalion, through the story of Prague's golem to the robot of Karel Capek, who coined the word, people have fantasised about the possibility of building intelligent machines," they wrote in a document, hoping to put across their point.

"Now that humankind stands on the threshold of an era when ever more sophisticated robots, bots, androids and other manifestations of artificial intelligence seem poised to unleash a new industrial revolution, which is likely to leave no stratum of society untouched, it is vitally important for the legislation to consider all its implications."

To better understand what those implications might be, I turn to Nick Bostrom, a Swedish philosopher at Oxford whose areas of study sound almost mythological and include "existential risk," the "anthropic principle," and "consequentialism." Your guess is as good as mine when it comes to what any of it actually means. I tried to contact Mr. Bostrom to no avail, but from the grim, Ingmar Bergman–like expression conveyed in his author photographs, it doesn't bode well for any of us.

Warnings that we might be forfeiting our dominant position to machines seem to triangulate among advanced-degree scientists operating primarily at three universities: MIT, Oxford, and Cambridge. Moving across the academic spectrum as I have done this past month, I have found that the impersonality of their knowledge is not very reassuring.

Nick Bostrom's recent book, *Superintelligence: Paths, Dangers, Strategies,* borrows heavily on the "be careful what you wish for" scenario. He argues that when fully realized, artificial intelligence might be humanity's undoing if not carefully managed beforehand, as in now. The titles of his papers do little to help calm nerves: "Existential Risks: Analyzing Human Extinction Scenarios and Related Hazards" requires a stiff drink or pharmaceuticals.

Want further proof that humanity might be ending itself soon? How about this: "Robots evolve quickly and efficiently after a virtual mass extinction modeled after real life disasters"? This claim comes from the University of Texas at Austin in a research article, "Extinction Events Can Accelerate Evolution." Its proposition is enough to persuade you to pour vodka over your breakfast cereal.

That Mr. Bostrom and most of his colleagues—looking equally despondent, by the way—are operating outside my educational boundaries fed my determination to locate someone who could explain the future clearly without sending me into a deep depression.

Wendell Wallach is such a person. Oxford University Press published his book *Moral Machines: Teaching Robots Right from Wrong.* I very much like the encouraging level of friendliness conveyed by the image on its front cover: it features a man and a robot shaking hands. Perhaps more important to me is that someone who knows his sister has reassured me that he is an "accessible intellect." I'm thrilled to learn that such a category of people exists.

It turns out that Mr. Wallach is many things: a senior adviser to the Hastings Center; an author of several books on the implications of advanced technology; and an expert on the ethical and governance concerns posed by emerging technologies, particularly artificial intelligence. He is affiliated with Yale University's Interdisciplinary Center for Bioethics. He is also a kind man who has invited me to lunch.

That lunch requires me to take a train to New Haven, Connecticut, where we've agreed to meet at the train station. So that Mr. Wallach would have no problem spotting me once I detrain, I send a brief description of my physical self as tall with reddish hair.

The train ride to New Haven passes alongside Bridgeport. It is a city that, settled by English colonists, developed into a major center of trade, shipbuilding, and whaling. The city was industrialized in the nineteenth century, and its economic mainstay was manufacturing. By 1930, Bridgeport was a thriving industrial center where Columbia Records built its main pressing plant.

America's deindustrialization in the 1970s sent Bridgeport into near bankruptcy, from whence it is still struggling to revitalize itself; the shells of hollowed-out buildings are sobering reminders of the fallout from industrial and technological revolutions.

I would guess, given the books he's written, that Wendell Wallach will soon inform me that we are in the middle of another technological revolution—one that will force upon us our greatest moral challenges.

MR. WALLACH IS where he needs to be to greet me at the New Haven train station. He is sporting a closely cropped white beard and wearing a casual jacket with no tie. From our correspondence, I know in advance that he will be taking me to a local restaurant—a quiet place, where our conversation will not be rushed. During the drive there, I try to explain myself, along with the purpose of my book. He listens politely with an air of gentle wariness. I have no idea what he is thinking.

"Here we are," he says as we pull up in front of a drab-looking building with no windows. "The entrance is in the back."

I follow him through the restaurant's counterintuitive front door.

Once we're inside, an Italian theme announces itself with mosaic tiles and plastic grape leaves. We are ushered to a secluded corner table.

Mr. Wallach is a regular at the restaurant, and there is genial chitchat with the waitress, who tells him that her dog— heartbroken when left behind in the house—is happy to wait for her in the car parked outside.

Determined to appear as intelligent as I am able, I forgo a glass of wine but offer one to him. I'm sorry he turns it down; it might have put us both more at ease. We are each handed a menu with pasta-inclined options. I follow Mr. Wallach's lead and order the same: homemade fettuccine in tomato sauce and roasted vegetables. Frank Sinatra is quietly crooning "In the Wee Small Hours of the Morning," while Mr. Wallach watches me haltingly test my tape recorder to make sure its volume works correctly. It will soon be clear to Mr. Wallach that I have no real grip on the topic at hand, and so I decide to take a deliberately general approach.

"There seems to be a technological inevitability to the world" is my open-ended comment.

"Yes, there is," agrees Mr. Wallach. "Technology will win out just as long as someone wants it and someone else is willing to pay for it."

His avuncular, soft-spoken voice seems at odds with the implications of what he's just said. Seeing my concern, he is quick to point out that while it's true that robots can harm people, encroach upon our freedoms, and threaten the employment of those likely replaced by them, robots can also be immeasurably helpful. In surgery, they can limit the scope of human error; they can trigger a detonating device miles away from personnel who would otherwise risk their lives attempting that deadly task. It's the possibility not so much that robots will slip the bonds of their inventors as that political forces will likely demand more and more of technology.

Margaret Atwood had told me that of course we will build robots but suggested that we begin to ask ourselves who the *we* actually are. According to the U.S. Department of Defense, one-third of current U.S. fighter strength is composed of robots. Right around the corner are lethal autonomous weapons. Drones are piloted by a person, while LAWs—computerized machines referred to as "killer robots" by their detractors—can select and fire upon targets on their own when activated. The growing numbers of them in combat will expose them to the kinds of ethical issues that humans dread. They will be less of an expense to mass-produce, and so will be more difficult to contain than nuclear weapons.

Mr. Wallach has been campaigning for years to ban LAWs. Their proponents, when asked who should be held morally accountable when machines kill people, insist that—much like a self-driving car programmed to avoid hitting a pedestrian—robotic weaponry will enable the avoidance of killing innocent civilians in a war zone. I gather this was not a convincing argument for what, presently, are over twenty thousand signers of a petition—some of the most important names in science and technology of which there are more than thirty-one hundred researchers in artificial intelligence—calling for a global ban. Their open letter describes a stark scenario of the future in its belief that "autonomous weapons are ideal for tasks such as assassination, destabilizing nations, subduing populations and killing an ethnic group."

There is another, separate list of AI researchers calling on a ban, some seventeen thousand, including Elon Musk and Stephen Hawking. Trying not to sound overwrought by what might easily be conceived as a deadly juggernaut beyond human control, I calm myself into an even-voiced next question for Mr. Wallach.

"Do you think we should be pursuing all facets of technology, regardless of the consequences?"

"If you don't explore everything, someone else will, not just in the military, but in all areas of life."

Mr. Wallach is of the belief that limiting scientific investigation has not proven to be a good idea but that we should limit what is deployed. This is easier said than done, he tells me.

"What are the moral ramifications?" I ask.

"Well, they could be any number of things," Mr. Wallach says in mellifluous tones. "It could be that we're inventing our species out of existence."

I tend to wear my emotions on my face, and at the moment I must be looking distressed enough for Mr. Wallach to feel the need to adjust what he's just said.

"The point is, we are in the midst of a tech storm of possibilities and now is the time for a conversation about which values we're putting into place right now, because those values probably lead to places very few people would condone."

I'm not sure whether I am being warned that ours is a future without hope, or if it's a message of reassurance: that if humankind were given half a chance, it might come to its collective senses. My conversation with Mr. Wallach is clumsy, with my taking three steps forward and stumbling back two. I start again.

"Do you think that core moral values are innate?"

"Yes, well, that's the question, isn't it? Are certain elements of morality intrinsic; or is it a utilitarian analysis: that certain aspects of morality have nothing to do with human nature? . . . Or it might be that they have something to do with human nature to the extent we're social animals and must find ways of functioning together."

"I've spent the last seven months contemplating those very questions, and I still have no idea" is what I say.

I feel that I've disappointed Mr. Wallach with an inadequate answer, and so I refocus our conversation on the premise of his book, the subtitle of which is *Teaching Robots Right from Wrong*. Mr. Wallach writes that given the rapid emergence of increasingly complex, autonomous software agents and robots, machines sensitive to ethical consideration (in other words, the factoring of ethical consideration into their choices) should no longer stay in the realm of science fiction. But after centuries of puzzling over what is morally acceptable, we have failed to describe it to ourselves. How, then, I ask Mr. Wallach, will we be able to program it into a computer? Who is it that does what to build moral robots?

"Initially, humans will be doing the teaching, and robots the learning," Mr. Wallach says.

I mean no disrespect, I tell Mr. Wallach, but the process he has just described is less than reassuring, given that humans have shown a repeated and sometimes-alarming inability to identify right from wrong.

"I understand your point" is his polite reply.

Our meal arrives. Twirling my pasta into small portions so there is enough time for me to speak between mouthfuls, I describe my conversation the previous month with Baroness Greenfield. Among her beliefs are that because the brain grows after birth, the connections it makes are mirrored, shaped, and strengthened to reflect one's unique experiences, that some part of thinking is a function of personality, that not only does one's thought process contribute to moral reasoning but emotions play an indispensable part. Emotions might be the enemy of reason, as Greek and Roman Stoics would have us believe. But emotions might also serve to hone virtuous character, as Aristotle proposed. Mr. Wallach agrees that it is a combination of emotion and reason that dictates the mechanics of moral behavior in ways not yet fully understood.

"So how do you program moral decision making in artificial intelligence when you're not sure how it happens in humans?" I ask.

His answer is to assemble a moral system starting with what is morally translatable to machines.

"But how does one decide what is morally translatable when morality is such a relative concept?" I ask.

Mr. Wallach looks put off, and it makes me embarrassed without knowing why I should be.

"You need to be careful about using the term 'relative.'"

"Okay, I'll rephrase the question. What do you think will happen in terms of the process of providing robots with a moral direction?"

"It will be done in very different ways. There will be a kind of Darwinian process to the various approaches. Certain approaches will actually succeed and become useful."

I ask if we should assume that robots will likely be programmed with moral directions that align with their country's own cultural take on morality. Should we assume that morality could be standardized?

"I don't know," he says. "I'm raising these issues now because there's a pragmatic need to do so sooner rather than later. Either we come up with some basic principles so that there's cohesion, or we won't function."

Our plates are cleared while more questions line up in my head: *Who comes up with these basic principles? And how would they be legislated?*

Technological advances in not only artificial intelligence and robotics but also biotechnology, nanotechnology, and neuroscience have left policy makers, business leaders, and the public facing ethical issues previously residing with moral philosophers. Though the prospects of superintelligence that may or may not threaten humanity appear to be decades away, by retreating from the hard decisions about our future, we leave behind a vacuum of moral agency. But it seems unrealistic to depend on government to make policy decisions when it comes to artificial intelligence when our politicians have proven incapable of agreeing on the most rudimentary issues, like health care.

"So whose morality will it be?" I ask Mr. Wallach. "Who decides on what goes into building a moral machine: the creators of the future? Because I've got to tell you, they seem to have their own thing going on. Ray Kurzweil. What's he all about?"

It was an ungainly transition to an important point I want to make. And, actually, I know something of what Ray Kurzweil is about. I know that he wrote a book over twenty-five years ago titled *The Age of Intelligent Machines* and, fifteen years later, one called *The Singularity Is Near,* which convinced my son, then ten, that homework was irrelevant because, eventually, everything would be taken care of in the merging of his physical self and advancing technology. I know that Kurzweil has convinced himself and others that something called radical life extension will outwit mortality. I know that his goal is to live until biotechnology is able to reprogram our inherited biology and that, if all goes according to plan, molecular nanotechnology will enable us to rebuild our bodies entirely to last forever.

"The key thing to understand about Ray is that he's afraid of dying," says Mr. Wallach.

"I'm not surprised," I say. "Nothing good comes of it—certainly not for the person dying."

"The timeline he's using is predicated on him being able to upload himself within his lifetime," Mr. Wallach informs me.

The lunch bill is paid, and we leave as we came in, through the back way.

The drive to the train station gives us the chance to square off with the fundamental fact that you can't program a computer or develop an app without a high IQ. I recount my various meetings with Larry Ellison, Oracle's co-founder, who, it happened, was also one of three people who provided the seed money to launch the magazine I started in Los Angeles. Even then, some twenty-five years ago, it was clear to me that Mr. Ellison was operating in a different neurological zone than I was. And like Mr. Kurzweil, Mr. Ellison doesn't believe there's a point to dying.

Mr. Wallach and I discuss Google's purchase of a start-up company in London that specializes in artificial intelligence for computers. The young founder—a chess master at the age of twelve—made his first fortune as a teenager by co-creating the video game *Theme Park,* a simulation game in which the player designs and operates an amusement park. More recently, he has led a study at University College London that scanned human brains and has found that a person's thoughts can be deducted from his or her neural activity. I'm not particularly comfortable with the idea of the creator of a video game called *Theme Park* bridging to thought prediction, but, unarguably, he is a very, very smart person.

With an important part of the future shaped by people who possess an extreme and specific kind of intelligence (borderline autistic, it's been suggested to me by some journalists), are these individuals operating at a morally abstracted distance from the masses that experience the effects of their technology?

I ask Mr. Wallach if he thinks the Ray Kurzweils of the world are taking us up to the brink of an ethic shift.

"You'll have to go see for yourself" are Mr. Wallach's last words to me before I take the train back to whatever was next.

23

SO WHO, EXACTLY, GETS TO SET THE NEW RULES?

Prediction is very difficult, especially if it's about the future.

—Niels Bohr

A summary of morality, as conceived by the legendary Seven Sages, who were early sixth-century B.C. philosophers, statesmen, and lawgivers, reads, "Control anger. Avoid injustice. Acknowledge religion. Control pleasure. Watch luck. Honor forethought. Grasp learning. Pursue repute. Act justly. Praise virtue."

A series of ten two-word aphorisms is easier composed than practiced. Inevitably, the number of ways we do things wrong exceeds the number of ways we do them right. We are, after all, only human.

That's the problem.

But that might also be our saving grace, for it can be said that the distinguishing feature of humankind is its capacity to right itself when things go too wrong.

So are things going too wrong?

It's difficult to believe otherwise when distrust has risen as much as diversity; when political parties are so polarized and there is a pervasive mistrust of institutions, including the church; when an American president, as a Nobel Peace Prize recipient, served two complete terms with his nation at war; when Europe, hit by the biggest migrant crisis in decades, has bargained with Turkey's dictatorial leader, who flouts human rights, to take back refugees seeking asylum in the EU in exchange for a multibillion-euro aid package; when homosexuality is punishable by death in certain cultures; and when, in Mosul, the jihadists' de facto capital of Iraq, nineteen women—who were taken as sex slaves by Islamic State fighters but who refused to have sex with them—were burned to death in cages in front of hundreds of people.

The daily news offers bleak, bitter reminders that ugly times breed ugly minds, but despite what seems to be an endless series of savagery, various graphs plotting wealth and our life expectancy—and, yes, even peace—say not. And though writing this book has forced me to acknowledge humankind's sometimes immoral scramble to prevail, I still believe that our resourcefulness, our ingenuity, and what I believe to be our godliness will ensure that things not go too wrong. And, yes, I am often of the mind that the Internet has impoverished the English language while playing host to the worst and weirdest in us all. At the same time I recognize that knowledge is accumulative, and I am keenly aware of the degree to which that knowledge can be so easily shared now. For this I give credit where credit is due: to the inventors of technology.

RAY KURZWEIL HAS been described as a "restless genius" by the *Wall Street Journal,* and his biography includes a great deal of information, including the facts that "aside from futurology, he is involved in fields such as optical character recognition . . . , text-to-text speech synthesis, [and] speech recognition technology."

Mr. Kurzweil has done a great deal for those of us who have no idea how technology actually works. This has made Mr. Kurzweil a very rich man.

There are quite a few very rich men—and a few women not as rich but rich nonetheless—residing in Silicon Valley, a place referred to as the greatest creation of entitlement in history.

The barons of high tech think of themselves as different from those on Wall Street. Their overweening confidence has provided them with a kind of neo-missionary zeal. Some of Silicon Valley's smartest and wealthiest people have embraced Singularitarianism, a movement defined in Mr. Kurzweil's best-selling book. It exposes the belief that a technological singularity—in other words, the creation of a superintelligence—will happen at some near point in the future.

Singularity University is close to Google headquarters in Mountain View. Google is a longtime supporter of Singularity University. Ray Kurzweil is a public advocate for the futurist and trans-humanist movements. He is committed to life extension technologies, and he has ties to Google. Google, lest we forget, is a publicly owned business.

Given the wholesale vacuuming up of Big Data, we might take time to deliberate on the issue of holding morally accountable the data gatherers with something to sell.

Google has a great deal to sell to those who can afford it.

I inquire about taking a tour of the Singularity campus, to speak to a former student, or to see the facilities in some fashion. I get back "We don't have anyone available for a tour so I'm afraid we need to decline."

I write once again and am advised of various paid programs: "We have forwarded your email to our Events Manager who can let you know of upcoming public events. We would also recommend subscribing to our newsletter here is the link http://singularityu.org this will also let you know of upcoming programs and dates."

Pulling whatever strings are within my reach, I contact an acquaintance, who was affiliated at one time with Singularity University and who is now an executive at a tech magazine. She informs me that unless the university can identify "revenue potential," it will not entertain visit suggestions. Having completely failed to breach the walls of Singularity University,

I set my sights on one of the notable leaders in the technology sector.

Martine Aliana Rothblatt is an entrepreneur and space law-yer who began her career as a man named Martin, first in the field of communications satellite law and then in life science projects such as the Human Genome Project. She was the cre-ator of GeoStar and Sirius Radio, and she is the founder and CEO of United Therapeutics, a biotechnology firm she estab-lished to find a treatment for pulmonary hypertension after her daughter was diagnosed with the disease. Dr. Rothblatt has made $38 million during what is coming up to my one year of searching for moral meaning.

When I inquire about meeting Dr. Rothblatt, this is what I receive from one of her assistants:

> *Dr. Rothblatt's location at any time is on a need-to-*
> *know basis. I am not privy to her schedule unless she has*
> *something scheduled with me or someone within the FL*
> *Terasem office. I'm sorry I am unable to be more specific*
> *at this time; she has different offices within the US.*

Under other circumstances, I might have hunted Dr. Roth-blatt to the ends of the earth out of sheer curiosity, but after several failed attempts to locate her, I decide my limited time might be more constructively spent at the Modern Cosmism Conference, which is scheduled this month at the New York Society for Ethical Culture.

COSMISM DESCRIBES ITSELF as "the integral, optimistic theory of human evolution where concepts of truth, reality, freedom and happiness will be deeply revised." Conceived some one hundred years ago in Russia, it is a futuristic, post-humanity concept, which banks on technological immortal-ity to enable highly moral, super-conscious beings that will colonize the universe. And like the trans-humanists Martine Rothblatt and Ray Kurzweil, those who believe in Cosmism consider the human body yesterday's technology and rely on scientific and technological advancements to enable immortality.

I certainly understand a hesitancy to accept that at death and with death we are gone completely. Trans-humanists are fiercely determined this will not be the case and focus on how to preempt it. Locating a trans-humanist online, I ask how this will happen. His return e-mail is confident but does not include directions: "It is about mind uploading, super intelligence, artificial consciousness, conditional immortality and our cosmic mission in distant future."

A week before attending the Modern Cosmism Conference, I receive information on its speakers, who include cosmologists, neuroscientists, philosophers, interdisciplinary researchers, and what are referred to as "protagonists of Trans-humanism."

I'm not surprised to see that one of the speakers is noted as "Advisor to Singularity University." I also see that Wendell Wallach is on the list, and so I am relieved to know that I'll not be cast entirely into the unknown.

"Ring me with a report as soon as you return," says Simon. "I want to know how technology will offer immortality when it can't manage to accurately predict the weather."

I arrive at the conference in time to hear one of the first speakers, a Dutch neuroscientist and former director of neuroengineering at the third-largest research organization in Europe. He pounds away on his thesis, and I am listening intently but have absolutely no idea what is meant by it.

The next speaker is an anxious-looking man whose topic is "Whole Brain Emulation and Neuromorphic Technology." His PowerPoint presentation clicks forward, one slide at a time, while he insists we are our neuro-connections.

I doubt it.

The human brain is composed of a hundred thousand cells,

all containing about ten billion neurons working together in an inexplicable way. It is the most complex of all biological expressions. One-fourth of our body's blood supply courses through its veins and arteries, making us who we are. I don't buy the idea that we are our connections. But the man is already on to a slide headlined "Mind Uploading." Its first bullet point is "Assumption: creating prosthetic neurons and connections is an essential aspect of brain building."

I don't buy that either: that mind uploading can transfer our personalities out of ourselves and into engineering substrates. By the time the final slide in his presentation appears referring to "Synthetic Realities," I can be heard rifling through my purse for aspirin.

The next speaker wastes no time before referring to the Akashic records, a compendium of thoughts, events, and emotions encoded in a nonphysical plane of existence—a hall of records that has noted and continues to register the life experience and desires of every human being from the beginning of time and the reactions to experience of all in the animal kingdom. Only a trained occultist can distinguish between actual experience and those astral pictures created by the imagination. So there's that.

The remainder of the morning is spent listening to various descriptions of a techno-utopia when human beings and machines will merge and superior intelligence will take altered forms. It seems to me an expensive and self-selecting proposition of cyborg immortality, one requiring the kind of wealth possessed by relatively few. I am hoping to ask about the moral obligation to use technology and innovation so that we might solve the problems here on earth first, but the lunch break is announced.

Wendell Wallach invites me to join a few others for a quick bite to eat at a Vietnamese restaurant not far away. James Hughes, another in the lunch group, is an afternoon speaker at the conference; his talk is titled "Cosmism, Moral Enhancement, and the Religious Dialogue with Transhumanism." At one time the executive director of the World Transhumanist Association, funded in part by the enigmatic Martine Roth-blatt, Mr. Hughes is a practicing Buddhist and speaks to me about his religious dialogue with trans-humanism. He believes that enlightenment can be reflected in the values and methods with which we master technology.

"I see," I tell him. Though I don't quite.

It is Mr. Wallach's talk that follows lunch, and he brings much-needed clarity to the multifaceted subject of transcendence by concentrating on scientifically inspired visions of the future.

Mr. Wallach asks us to consider who we are versus what we want to be. And taking a bottom-up engineering approach to what it means to be human, he suggests that consciousness has to be something more than digital programming.

The more Mr. Wallach talks, the more I am in agreement. Expressing a disquiet about the direction of research and our increasing reliance on complex systems and the acceleration of innovation, Mr. Wallach is somewhat critical of the notion of moral enhancement—the idea we can enhance human moral decisions neuro-pharmaceutically. He cites Propranolol, a drug for high blood pressure, which also reduces implicit racial bias, and Oxytocin, a hormone that reduces labor pains, which is also known to increase bonds between mother and infant.

There are drugs developed to counter debilitating diseases of the mind, which are in demand by the healthy who use them as cognitive enhancers. Smart drugs work by altering the supplies of neurotransmitters that affect the brain. They modify neurochemical supplies by reducing noise levels and allowing signals in the brain to be clearer, thus increasing the quality of information flow in the brain. How soon will it be, I wonder, before a drug test is a natural precondition for a job interview in order to ensure a level playing field?

Research has proven that moral behavior changes during the course of twelve waking hours, and—regardless of our cultural background—we are all more susceptible to whatever constitutes immorality in the late afternoon.

All of these issues raise the question of whether moral accountability is, in part or in whole, a scientific issue. More to the point, when does brain science free us from personal responsibility for our actions?

Finally comes the conference's question-and-answer session. I take a close look at those in the audience. They strike me as less interested in the world we are in than the one they want. Predominantly male, most of them, it appears, have not had the time or inclination to shave successfully, and they are wearing a variety of consistently dubious knitwear.

Despite the clubfooted use of the English language that I've had to endure for the better part of the last two hours, the conference has put forth philosophical issues arising from a future that will include artificial consciousness and mind uploading, both of which will render personal appearances beside the point. And so I feel confident that with the impressive number of advanced degrees in the room the questions from the audience will be interesting ones.

I'm curious to learn, for example, if there will be limits to our artificial capacities and the functional simulations we will create, and I am eager to hear how our concepts of subjectivity, perception, and morality will change if and when we live in the virtual reality of a mega-consciousness environment where individuals can experience multiple, genderless personalities.

The first question from the audience is no question at all but a prepared statement.

"I don't think people who've committed suicide should be allowed to come back."

After a year of trying to sort through what might be in store for morality, I am delighted that subjective judgments will continue to be made in the infinite future—no matter where in the galaxies one's downloaded self happens to be.

24

WHEREIN I CONCLUDE BY LOOKING FORWARD

Sometimes a deep question is better than a straight answer.

—*Werner Herzog, German filmmaker*

Shortly after I return to London from New York, Simon and I have another one of our lunches.

"Are you done yet?" he asks.

"With what?"

"Your quixotic search for morality."

Granted, I tend to make a thing more grand or nostalgic than it actually is. Admittedly, I sometimes exile my intelligence to a self-imposed denial of facts in order to avoid being disappointed. It's also true that, when romanticism leaks through what should be a reason-sealed perspective, my logical self is often flooded by sentimentality. So, in that sense, I can be quixotic. As I am admitting to Simon that, despite a year spent canvassing for morality, my campaign—replete with false starts and hand-brake stops—was leading me nowhere, my expression of minor worry gives way to something more emotional.

"What kind of world is it when ISIS leaders are blessing the slaughter of innocents, migrants are left to drown at sea, and property values are all that seem to matter!" I blurt out. "Mass killings in Paris, Putin, and now Trump—all in one year!"

"I agree; it's not been an ideal year to locate morality," says

Simon, with more empathy than I would have expected. "But timing isn't your problem."

"Alright, enlighten me."

"The problem is that you're directionally challenged."

"What in the hell is that supposed to mean?" I ask belligerently.

"You're using an old map. You need a new one, and then you need to enlist someone young enough to teach you how to read it."

The next day, having stepped back from my emotions, I come to the conclusion that Simon has a point: the age I am has placed me squarely in what Henry James called "the country of the general lost freshness."

DETERMINED NOT TO be held back by a self-preserving perspective, I recruit seven young men and women to snap at my beleaguered heels. These twentysomethings agree to meet in the front room of my apartment every other Sunday afternoon.

Monica, who has organized the group, is a student at the Philosophy and Theology College within the University of London. Krystof, with a law degree from Harvard, is doing his PhD research at the London School of Economics on the rule of law and unjust enrichment. Johannes, whose postdoctoral study is taking place in the department of philosophy at the Humboldt University of Berlin, is interested in environmental ethics. Asbjorn, an Oxford graduate, is conducting PhD research in the area of distributive justice. Jean, having attended McGill University in Quebec and Oxford, is a lawyer focused on ethical problems in pediatric medicine. Polly has a degree from Cambridge; her PhD research includes bioethics and philosophical pragmatism. Stuart, the oldest of the group, is an academic with a career in the financial sector whose PhD research concerns the philosophical problems in finance. He's interested in how, during the creation of financial institutions, they may or may not be affected by moral considerations. Having worked in media as a journalist and editor, he now runs a research company whose clients number hedge funds and banks.

Until recently, a generation was measured in twenty-year increments. With technology hurling trends ahead, twenty years is now considered too long, and so generations are more typically defined by the impactful factors during shorter and shorter time periods. These seven young people meeting with me fall into what is referred to among market researchers like Jane Buckingham as Generation Y.

"Our generation had only a few signs of what constituted right and wrong," Ms. Buckingham told me some six months prior, while discussing the possible evolutionary advantages of future generations. "Young people today are exposed to so much, so quickly, and they have so much to process: it could be that the perspective of our generation might just be an antiquated way of looking at today's world . . . and that young people today can deal with it all."

If my group of seven is an accurate representation, their generation seems to be dealing with "it all" with disarming confidence; some would label it entitlement. They don't accept the world as it is offered to them, and none hesitate to question the status quo of organized groups, be they religions, businesses, or governments. When it comes to what is societally and institutionally expected of them, the first thing they are likely to do is to consider whether it is consistent with their personal perception of morality. This might explain why the majority of the generation above me disparages Edward Snowden—the former National Security Agency contractor who handed over Western government secrets to the press—while most in the generation below me believe he acted with moral fortitude.

I believe in the lasting power that comes from habit. If we develop and adhere to habits of respect, for example, we become more respectful, and if we become more respectful, we become better people through application. This is the modus vivendi that sustains my thinking. But while I am rigidly insisting that one be put through the rigors of morality, not unlike insisting that one be able to do long division in order to solve a math problem, the solution for this group of seven young people is simply to reach for a calculator. What they seem to possess—lacking in me—is the ability to recognize a flexible concept of morality. Theirs is a 360-degree moral view, sourced by anyone in the public eye: politicians, people with big followings on social media, YouTube stars, sports stars, and celebrities.

They tell me that there are clear evolutionary reasons why humankind does what it does, but what matters is not so much our nature as the outcome of our actions: that there are values and virtues that should be considered universal, but the ways in which those values and virtues express themselves are not always the same.

They tell me that to understand our own moral codes, we must first ask who is challenging them. They are comfortable with a multicultural society and remind me that the issues facing the world today are not confined to national boundaries, that the world is interconnected and we need to understand it as a whole, that to believe ours is the only morality is unworldly, that at times we must be willing to adjust our own definition of morality.

They tell me that elected leaders have been unable to inspire morality in any consistent way. America is fraying. Europe is stalled in a traffic jam of immigrants and refugees. Russia bullies in every deadly direction. There's a gaping, open wound between means and ends in the Middle East, while radicalization takes flight on social media. They say that the world today is now one of less-bad options. They tell me that we in the West must find it in ourselves to confront an incredibly challenging question: What will anchor us in our own distinct morals and ethics and at the same time yield to the fact there are other distinct cultures with different moral, ethical, and religious systems? They tell me that in order to contemplate this—in order to retain that crucial, self-questioning stance, both as individuals and as a society—we'll need to take our eyes off the mirror in front of us and look squarely at people with different truths and values, because only then will we be able to make the difficult decisions of when to be tolerant. They tell me that at times those decisions will require us to relinquish some part of our moral ground, and at other times they will call on us to protect the moral ground we are determined to hold. Out of such decisions will arise moral systems that will enable us to navigate the future of what they perceive to be a conflicted, heaving world. They tell me what I already know: that I am hardwired with moral absolutes while they believe that morality exists in the broader scope and consideration of people, current events, and social power.

"Mankind should have learned by now that you can't be an absolutist when it comes to morality," says Stuart. "We need only look at our past to know that the preexisting concepts of morality have often been corrupt and immoral and, fortunately, rejected."

Stuart is results oriented in a way I appreciate, and he agrees to lead us through what might otherwise be a treacherous landscape by suggesting that our moral map include three topographical peaks: one is the utilitarian idea of how much good is created in society; another is rights based, the school of thought that contends that even if it makes people feel good, there are things you nonetheless cannot do; the third has to do with virtue, where there is no enforced obligation to be good, but—simply put—there are ways of being that are good to be.

"WHERE ON THE map is the starting point?" I ask him. "Does it begin with human nature or the outcome of human nature? Do we look at what people do and reverse engineer a sense of morality, or do we insist on doing the right thing?"

The others are eager to join, and spontaneous enthusiasm flashes on and off like naked lightbulbs. They suggest that there are two versions of morality in the world today: one has to do with the pursuit of it and its virtue; a second has to do with the realistic application of it.

"So should I visualize the two coordinates as latitude and longitude?" I ask.

The group has its say. "That's right," they tell me, sounding triumphant.

And then they tell me something else. Something unforgettable.

They tell me that in uncharted territory where the two coordinates converge is usually the right way to treat another human being: at that convergence—somewhere in the nexus between reason, emotion, and will—morality is most likely found, along with hope.

EPILOGUE

Out beyond ideas of wrongdoing and
rightdoing there is a field.
I'll meet you there.

—*Rumi, thirteenth-century Persian theologian*

Erwin James revealed his family name to be Monahan. He is now a trustee of the Prison Reform Trust, as well as a fellow of the Royal Society for the Encouragement of Arts. He is also a patron of a charity that promotes the arts among the marginalized and of a social enterprise that trains and employs ex-offenders. Currently, he writes for the *Guardian*.

The chairman of Volkswagen admitted that the decision by employees to cheat on emission tests was made when it became apparent that they would be unable to meet the U.S. clean air standards. This occurred more than a decade ago. As a result of the growing cost of the scandal, the company reported the biggest annual loss in its seventy-nine-year history and agreed to settle for $14.7 billion.

THE ROYAL BANK of Scotland put aside an extra £2 billion to cover the cost of "cleaning up" past scandals. Embedding personal responsibility in firms and banks among their executives, the head of the U.K.'s Financial Conduct Authority has enacted changes that assign legal responsibility for decisions made by senior managers.

After Michael Woodford blew the whistle on Olympus—not right away, but eventually—the company's chairman was charged with accounting fraud; he pleaded guilty and received a five-year suspended sentence.

The *Financial Times* was sold to the Japanese media group Nikkei for $1.3 billion. Lionel Barber remains its editor. Though the *FT*'s editorial independence was key to the negotiations, Michael Woodford voiced his concern over Nikkei's hesitation when it has come to hard-hitting corporate coverage and likened it to the "public relations office for Olympus . . . in contrast to the *FT*, which broke the news."

To curb prostitution in France, its parliament voted to punish the client with fines of up to €1,500, with those convicted ordered to attend classes on the plight of prostitutes. In a reversal of legal burden, the National Assembly also abolished a law that penalized prostitutes for "passively soliciting" in public.

Across Europe authoritarian parties have gained momentum and helped elect ultranationalist governments in Hungary and Poland. In the Netherlands and Sweden, centralist parties have banned together in an attempt to prevent this same fate.

Sadiq Khan, the Muslim son of a London bus driver, became the mayor of London. During his campaign, he explained himself simply: "I'm a Londoner, I'm a European, I'm British, I'm English, I'm of Islamic faith, of Asian origin, of Pakistani heritage, a dad, a husband."

Six months after failing to win a parliamentarian majority—which interrupted the thirteen-year, single-party rule of his Islamic-rooted party—President Recep Tayyip Erdogan intervened to prevent the formation of a coalition government. In between the elections, he delivered divisive rhetoric and renewed the fighting in the southeast between Turkish forces and an outlawed Kurdish group. He has widened Turkey's terror laws to include the actions of journalists, charity workers,

opposition politicians, and more; and, after a failed coup, he
detained, dismissed, suspended or arrested some 35,000 people
who included, among others, members of military, education
ministry, and the judiciary.

Traveling to refugee camps housing Kurdish women who
have survived the brutalities of ISIS, Rojin has launched a program that provides psychological support and training courses
for skills in the workforce. She still sings.

Noel Biderman insisted that even after hackers leaked personal data on and about Ashley Madison clients, a substantial
number of new clients have signed on to the site. The company
countered reports accusing the site of having fewer genuine
female users than was promoted, saying internal data released
by hackers had been incorrectly analyzed.

Unlike Ashley Madison's parent company, Tinder's parent
company, Match Group, has made a successful initial public offering. Investment money has been made available to
another, unrelated company, 3nder, which is, in effect, Tinder
for threesomes.

With no rolling back the technology that enables the free
distribution of pornography, Danish sex educators are now
openly discussing pornography in the classrooms, enabling

children and young people to understand that sex is about people and pornography is about bodies. They believe that an understanding that one is not the other will facilitate a broader dialogue that includes body image, self-esteem, and the meaning of consent.

Jacqueline Davis's company, Optimal Risk Management Ltd., which specializes in matters of security, is now teaching company personnel the basic principles of what to do in the event of a terrorist attack.

British women, looking for a man to father their child, are now able to select a sperm donor by using a mobile phone app allowing them to browse candidates based on desired physical characteristics. Once the donor is chosen, payment is made via the app, which delivers the sperm to the fertility clinic where the woman is being treated. Women can also set up a "wish list" on the app, which will alert them when a donor with the selected characteristics becomes available.

India—a "surrogacy hub" for paying, childless couples whose own countries have made commercial surrogacy illegal—has unveiled a draft law stipulating that only local infertile couples, married for at least five years, could seek a woman to act as surrogate, and she must be a close relative.

In a bid to reverse its nation's aging workforce, China's Communist Party ended the nation's decades-long one-child policy. Married couples are allowed to have two children.

After a legal threat, the U.K.'s National Health Care System announced it will reconsider a decision to abandon the rollout of HIV-preventing PrEP drugs to gay men.

Wendell Wallach continues to argue against lethal autonomous weapons, including at the UN in Geneva. His most recent book is titled *A Dangerous Master: How to Keep Technology from Slipping Beyond Our Control*.

Ending a standoff with a sniper suspected of killing five of its officers on duty at a rally, the Dallas Police Department blew him up using a robot. British surgeons successfully performed the world's first robotic operation inside the eye, potentially revolutionizing the method by which certain medical conditions are treated.

Martine Rothblatt commissioned the creation of the "social robot" Bina48, which is able to carry on a conversation (of sorts). The robot's personality and appearance are based on Ms. Rothblatt's living spouse; they have stayed together since Ms. Rothblatt's sex-change operation. Its creator, David Hanson of Hanson Robotics, insists that humanoid robots can be genuine emotional companions.

Alphabet Inc., Google's parent company, was listed in a report from the Church of England as one of the church's "20 most valuable equity holdings," despite the church's commitment to confront companies accused of tax avoidance.

THE AMERICAN CIVIL Liberties Union filed a suit to obtain records concerning the legal basis for the use of lethal force outside conventional war zones. Its director warned, "There is great damage to the rule of law and human rights law when the United States, of all countries, engages in killings based on secret interpretations of the law or entirely new and unilateral legal frameworks outside the agreed-upon international framework that places important constraints upon lethal force and protects the right to life."

Waiting until the end of its two terms in office, the Obama administration revealed an estimated number of civilians killed since 2009 in 473 counterterrorism air strikes to be between 64 and 116. Simultaneously, a presidential order was issued calling on the government to adopt stricter guidelines, which would presumably reduce that risk.

The U.K. exited the European Union. The following day, the prime minister resigned, and within a remarkably short period of time Theresa May replaced him, whereupon one of the papers wrote, "What makes a May premiership interestingly unpredictable is that she has always been driven less by ideology than by morality, a very personal sense of right or wrong."

In a stunning repudiation of the Establishment, Americans have elected as their president Donald Trump, who has rewritten the rules. Time will reveal how he is judged. But if it is true that our collective morality reflects the behavioral standards by which we submit ourselves to others, then he has succeeded already in reimaging a nation.

NOTES AND ADDITIONAL READING

PROLOGUE

The Analects of Confucius (Lulu Press, 2013).

Michael Puett and Christine Gross-Loh, *The Path: A New Way to Think About Everything* (Viking, 2017).

CHAPTER ONE: WHEREIN I BEGIN WITH
THE DEFINITION OF THE WORD

The London Library, http://www.londonlibrary.co.uk/.

CHAPTER TWO: ACCORDING TO A CONVICTED
MURDERER, IT HAS TO DO WITH CHARACTER

Laura Bates, *Shakespeare Saved My Life: Ten Years in Solitary with the Bard* (Sourcebooks, 2013).

Erwin James, *A Life Inside: A Prisoner's Notebook* (Guardian Books, 2003).

William McDougall, *Character and the Conduct of Life* (Methuen, 1944).

Stephen Reid, *A Crowbar in the Buddhist Garden* (Thistledown Press, 2012).

CHAPTER THREE: A NEUROSCIENTIST EXPLAINS
THE EVOLUTIONARY ORIGINS OF MORALITY

Molly Crockett, Crockett Lab, http://www.crockettlab.org/.

Charles Darwin, *The Origin of the Species* (Signet Classics, 2003).

Sam Harris, *The Moral Landscape: How Science Can Determine Human Values* (Free Press, 2010).

Alexander von Humboldt, *Views of Nature,* ed. Stephen T. Jackson and Laura Dassow Walls, trans. Mark W. Person (University of Chicago Press, 2014).

H. L. Mencken, *Treatise on Right and Wrong* (Kegan Paul, Trench, Trubner, 1934).

Steven Pinker, "The False Allure of Group Selection," *Edge,* June 18, 2012.

Ben Thompson, ed., *Ban this Filth! Letters from Mary Whitehouse* (Faber & Faber, 2012).

Robert Trivers, *Deceit and Self-Deception: Fooling Yourself the Better to Fool Others* (Penguin Books, 2011).

Edward O. Wilson, *The Meaning of Human Existence* (W. W. Norton, 2014).

CHAPTER FOUR: A BRIEF HISTORY OF MANKIND'S ATTEMPTS TO REIN IN BAD BEHAVIOR

Aristotle, *The Nicomachean Ethics,* trans. Jonathan Barnes (Penguin Classics, 2004).

Emily Benson, "Human Sacrifice May Have Helped Societies Become More Complex," *Science,* April 4, 2016.

Richard Dawkins, https://richarddawkins.net/.

John Ferguson, *Morals and Values in Ancient Greece* (Bristol Classical Press, 1989).

David Noel Freedman, ed., *Eerdmans Dictionary of the Bible* (Eerdman, 2000).

Kenneth Sylvan Guthrie, comp. and trans., *The Pythagorean Sourcebook and Library: An Anthology of Ancient Writings Which Relate to Pythagoras and Pythagorean Philosophy* (Phanes, 1987).

Edith Hamilton, *Mythology: Timeless Tales of Gods and Heroes* (Little, Brown, 1999).

The Koran (Cosimo Classics, 2010).

William Edward Hartpole Lecky, *History of European Morals from Augustus to Charlemagne* (D. Appleton, 1876).

Iris Murdoch, *The Sovereignty of Good* (Schocken Books, 1970).

Works by Plato, http://classics.mit.edu/Browse/browse-Plato.html.

Benjamin Rand, *The Classical Moralists* (Houghton Mifflin, 1909).

Jean-Jacques Rousseau, *Collected Writings of Rousseau,* ed. Roger Masters and Christopher Kelly, 13 vols. (published for Dartmouth College by University Press of New England, 1990–2010).

E. Hershey Sneath, ed., *The Evolution of Ethics: As Revealed in the Great Religions* (Yale University Press, 1927).

For Vedic hymns in Sanskrit, see Mantra Pushpam, https://www.youtube.com/watch?v=-yS-Jky997Y.

Robert Wright, *The Moral Animal: Why We Are the Way We Are: The New Science of Evolutionary Psychology* (Vintage Books, 1995).

CHAPTER FIVE: THE EDITOR OF THE *FINANCIAL TIMES*
PROVIDES A COST-BENEFIT ANALYSIS OF PRINCIPLES

Alan Page Fiske, *Structures of Social Life: The Four Elementary Forms of Human Relations* (Free Press, 1993).

Ian Morris, *Foragers, Farmers, and Fossil Fuels: How Human Values Evolve* (Princeton University Press, 2015).

CHAPTER SIX: INSTRUCTIONS ON HOW NOT TO CHEAT

To take the MoralDNA™ test, go to http://moraldna.org/.

CHAPTER SEVEN: PROS AND CONS OF DOING THE RIGHT THING

Michael Woodford, *Exposure: From President to Whistleblower at Olympus* (Penguin Books, 2013).

CHAPTER EIGHT: THE LAW: TOOLS OF CONTROL,
OR INSTRUMENTS OF ENLIGHTENMENT?

Sydney Biddle Barrows, *The Mayflower Madam: The Secret Life of Sydney Biddle Barrows* (Arbor House, 1986).

Jeremy Bentham, *The Principles of Morals and Legislation* (Prometheus Books, 1988).

Albert Camus, *The Rebel* (Penguin Books, 1984).

Owen Chadwick, *The Secularization of the European Mind in the Nineteenth Century* (Cambridge University Press, 1975).

Cicero, *On Duties* (Cambridge University Press, 1991).

Gertrude Himmelfarb, *The Moral Imagination: From Edmund Burke to Lionel Trilling* (Souvenir Press, 2006).

The Journal of Experimental Psychology, http://www.apa.org/pubs/journals
/xge/.

Atticus Lish, *Preparation for the Next Life* (OneWorld, 2015).

Hans-Georg Moeller, *The Moral Fool: A Case for Amorality* (Columbia
University Press, 2009).

Arthur Schopenhauer, *The Two Fundamental Problems of Ethics* (Oxford
World Classics, 2010).

H. G. Wells, *First and Last Things: A Confession of Faith and the Rule of
Law* (G. P. Putnam's Sons, 1908).

CHAPTER NINE: THE POLITICAL FUNCTION OF ETHICS

Babafemi A. Badejo, *Raila Odinga: An Enigma in Kenyan Politics* (Yintab
Books, 2006).

CHAPTER TEN: MONOGAMY (NOT SO MUCH ANYMORE)

Diane Ackerman, *A Natural History of Love* (Random House, 1994).

Niles Eldredge, *Why We Do It: Rethinking Sex and the Selfish Gene* (W. W.
Norton, 2004).

Stendhal, *On Love* (Hesperus, 2009). First published in French, 1822.

CHAPTER ELEVEN: THE SCREEN AS A SIREN

Homer, *The Iliad* (Penguin Classics, 2003).

Lewis Hyde, *Trickster Makes This World: Mischief, Myth, and Art* (Farrar,
Straus and Giroux, 1999).

George Bernard Shaw, *Man and Superman* (Penguin Classics, 1946).

Robert Weiss and Jennifer P. Schneider, *Always Turned On: Sex Addiction
in the Digital Age* (Gentle Path Press, 2015).

CHAPTER TWELVE: TESTOSTERONE: MORALITY'S
ENEMY, AS WELL AS ITS HERO

Stephen Banks, *Duels and Dueling* (Shire Library, 2012).

Thomas Bulfinch, *The Age of Chivalry* (Kindle edition online).

CHAPTER THIRTEEN: IMMORAL WOMEN: OR
JUST THOSE HAVING A BETTER TIME?

Marguerite Duras, *The Lover,* trans. Barbara Bray (Pantheon Books, 1985). Published in French as *L'amant.*

E. L. James, *Fifty Shades of Grey as Told by Christian* (Vintage Books, 2015).

Margaret Fox Schmidt, *Passion's Child: The Extraordinary Life of Jane Digby* (Hamish Hamilton, 1977).

CHAPTER FOURTEEN: CELEBRITIES AS STANDARD-BEARERS

Jean Baudrillard, *The Consumer Society: Myths and Structures,* trans. Chris Turner (Sage, 1998).

Leo Braudy, *The Frenzy of Renown: Fame and Its History* (Oxford University Press, 1986).

Geoffrey Chaucer, *The Complete Works of Geoffrey Chaucer,* vol. 3, *The House of Fame, The Legend of Good Women, The Treatise on the Astrolabe, An Account of the Sources of the Canterbury Tales,* ed. Walter W. Skeat (Clarendon Press, 1899).

Chong Ju Choi and Ron Berger, "Ethics of Celebrities and Their Increasing Influence in 21st Century Society," *Journal of Business Ethics* 91, no. 3 (Feb. 2010): 313–18.

Alison Jackson, *Alison Jackson: Confidential: What You See in This Book Is Not "Real"* (Taschen, 2007).

Steven Johnson, *Everything Bad Is Good for You: How Today's Popular Culture Is Actually Making Us Smarter* (Penguin Books, 2005).

Kim Kardashian West, *Selfish* (Rizzoli, 2015).

CHAPTER FIFTEEN: REALITY REDEFINED

Jane Buckingham, *What's Next: Predictions from 50 of America's Most Compelling People* (HarperCollins, 2008).

Peggy Orenstein, *Girls & Sex: Navigating the Complicated New Landscape* (HarperCollins, 2016).

CHAPTER SIXTEEN: THE WEB WONDERS
WHAT'S SO GREAT ABOUT THE TRUTH

Susan Greenfield, *Mind Change: How Digital Technologies Are Leaving Their Mark on Our Brains* (Rider, 2015).

Eric Zimmerman, http://ericzimmerman.com/.

CHAPTER SEVENTEEN: ETHICALLY SANITIZED WARFARE

Carl von Clausewitz, *On War* (Wordsworth, 1997).

David Rodin, https://www.youtube.com/watch?v=p-2Z0FsViJE.

CHAPTER EIGHTEEN: IMMORALITY'S BLACK SUN

Tadeusz Borowski, *This Way for the Gas, Ladies and Gentlemen* (Penguin Books, 1976).

A Brief History of Genocide, https://www.youtube.com/watch?v=K1g W23pFrQw.

Eric Hoffer, *The True Believer: Thoughts on the Nature of Mass Movements* (HarperCollins, 1951).

Lord Russell of Liverpool, *The Scourge of the Swastika: A Short History of Nazi War Crimes* (Frontline Books, 2013).

Philippe Sands, *East West Street: On the Origins of Genocide and Crimes Against Humanity* (Weidenfeld & Nicolson, 2016).

Bernhard Schlink, *Guilt About the Past* (Anansi, 2010).

CHAPTER NINETEEN: THE MORAL VAGARIES OF MAKING BABIES

Randi Hutter Epstein, *Get Me Out: A History of Childbirth from the Garden of Eden to the Sperm Bank* (W. W. Norton, 2010).

CHAPTER TWENTY: MAPPING A POST-GAY CULTURE

Robert Hofler, *Sexplosion: From Andy Warhol to "A Clockwork Orange"— How a Generation of Pop Rebels Broke All the Taboos* (HarperCollins, 2014).

Camille Paglia, *Vamps & Tramps* (Vintage Books, 1994).

Jeffrey Weeks, *The World We Have Won* (Routledge, 2007).

CHAPTER TWENTY-ONE: IS IT PROGRESS
IF WE BARTER WITH ETHICS?

Margaret Atwood, *The Handmaid's Tale* (McClelland and Stewart, 1985).

Barry Lord, *Art and Energy: How Culture Changes* (American Alliance of Museums Press, 2014).

CHAPTER TWENTY-TWO: PROGRAMMING MORALITY
IN ROBOTS (THEY'LL SHOW US HOW)

For the ban on lethal autonomous weapons, see the website of the Future of Life Institute, http://futureoflife.org.

Nick Bostrom, *Superintelligence: Paths, Dangers, Strategies* (Oxford University Press, 2014).

Wendell Wallach and Colin Allen, *Moral Machines: Teaching Robots Right from Wrong* (Oxford University Press, 2009).

CHAPTER TWENTY-THREE: SO WHO, EXACTLY,
GETS TO SET THE NEW RULES?

Greg Egan, *Permutation City,* 2nd ed., ebook published by author.

Ray Kurzweil, *The Singularity Is Near: When Humans Transcend Biology* (Gerald Duckworth, 2006).

ACKNOWLEDGMENTS

I thank all interviewed for this book. Their contributions were invaluable.

I am especially indebted to Lynn Nesbit, Nan Talese, and Daniel Meyer; to Rebecca Carter, Jack Hanbury-Tenison, and Monica Achieng-Ogola.

My dutiful appreciation to the *Economist,* the *Financial Times, The New Yorker,* and the *New York Times* for their coverage on moral issues during the time I wrote this book. I am grateful as well to the Athenaeum Club Library in London, the London Library, Oxford's Bodleian Library, the New York Public Library, and the New York Society Library.

My thanks are also due to those who have been generous with their time and encouragement. In Los Angeles, to Ann Louise Bardach, Allan Mayer, Kim and Michael McCarty, and Holly Palance.

In Istanbul, to Zuhal Kurt and Özlem Zengin.

In New York, to Eileen Bresnahan-Morgan, Peter Brown, Ruth Charny, Sara Colleton, Nancy Collins, Blythe Danner, Randi Epstein, Amanda Foreman, Wayne Lawson, Gilbert C. Maurer, Edward Miller, Frances Mitchell, Monina von Opel, Lisa Immordino Vreeland, and Angus Wilkie.

In Munich, to Jürgen Todenhöfer.

In Beijing, to Gilliam Collinsworth Hamilton.

In London, to Lionel de Rothschild, Peter Eyre, Ralph Fiennes, Virginia Fraser, Victoria Greenwood, Edwina Grosvenor, Mathias Hink, Dominic Hobson, Robert Noel, Deborah Owen, and Andrea Wong.